BULLY FREE®

BULLETIN BOARDS, POSTERS, AND BANNERS

Creative Displays for a Bully Free Classroom®, Grades K–8

ALLAN L. BEANE, PH.D., AND LINDA BEANE

free spirit
PUBLISHING®

The Library of Congress has cataloged the previous edition as follows:
Beane, Allan L., 1950-
    Bully free bulletin boards, posters, and banners : creative displays for a safe and caring school, grades K/8 / Allan L. Beane and Linda Beane.
        p. cm.
    ISBN 1-57542-186-0
1. Bullying in schools—Prevention. 2. Bullying in schools—Posters. 3. Bulletin boards. I. Beane, Linda. II. Title.
    LB3013.3.B42 2005
    371.5′8—dc22

                                                                        2005019090

Dedication
This book is dedicated to our son, Curtis Allan Beane, who was bullied in seventh grade and high school. It is also dedicated to our granddaughters, Emily Grace Turner and Sarah Gail Turner. Emily was born on the first anniversary of Curtis' death. She and Sarah have brought light into our darkness. It is our wish that this book and those who use it will bring light into the darkness of children who are mistreated.

Acknowledgments
Grateful thanks are offered to everyone who has helped by providing advice, information, and comments during the preparation of this book. We want to thank Free Spirit Publishing for believing in the project, and we are especially thankful for Douglas Fehlen's encouragement during the development process and for his editing contributions. We are also grateful to Judy Galbraith for her support of Bully Free® materials, and to Michele Dettloff and Marieka Heinlen for their fine illustration and design work on the book.

Edited by Douglas J. Fehlen
Cover design by Marieka Heinlen
Interior design by Michele Dettloff

10 9 8 7 6 5 4 3
Printed in the United States of America

Free Spirit Publishing Inc.
217 Fifth Avenue North, Suite 200
Minneapolis, MN 55401-1299
(612) 338-2068
help4kids@freespirit.com
www.freespirit.com

CONTENTS

INTRODUCTION

Bullying is one of the most severe and widespread problems facing today's schools. Despite heightened awareness of the problem and government initiatives dedicated to stopping it, bullying continues to occur at schools on a daily basis. News reports and references in popular culture only serve to reaffirm what most students, parents, and educators already know—bullying is a damaging fact of life that needs to be addressed. In fact, it is the most common form of school violence.

Bullying was once viewed as a "normal" part of growing up. Being threatened, harassed, and physically abused is not normal—it's dysfunctional and wrong. More student health problems and an increase in school violence—often involving young people retaliating against prolonged mistreatment—suggest that normalizing bullying has not lessened its effects. And while images from high-profile acts of violence in schools are horrifying, the effects of bullying extend far beyond major incidents that receive widespread media coverage. Bullying:

- creates a fearful school climate.
- leads to absenteeism.
- is a cause of loneliness, depression, post-traumatic stress, severe anxiety, substance abuse, and eating disorders in youth.
- increases the risk of suicide.
- negatively impacts learning.
- encourages membership in gangs, cults, and hate groups.
- affects everyone at school—those who are bullied, those who bully, and those who see bullying occur.

As an educator, you can help promote safe, supportive, and caring learning environments where all students have a sense of belonging and are able to achieve their best. Whether your school already has an anti-bullying program in place or you are making an individual effort to improve the school environment, this book can help.

Enlisting the involvement of students and staff, you can create displays that bring awareness to the problem of bullying and send the message that it will not be tolerated in classrooms, hallways, media centers, lunchrooms, locker rooms, or restrooms—or on buses, playgrounds, and other school areas. Creating these displays allows everyone to get involved. Start in your classroom, guidance office, or other school setting and move on to other areas. Encourage other staff members to participate in creating displays with their students so that anti-bullying messages can be seen throughout your school.

Bringing attention to bullying and taking steps to prevent it can have a profound impact upon an entire school or district. Students who have bullied begin to see how destructive it can be. Those who have been bullied feel safer knowing that the bullying will not be tolerated. At the same time, students who witness bullying—bystanders—feel empowered to speak out against bullying and report it when they see it. Everyone at school—students and staff—can work together toward creating a peaceful, bully free school where all feel accepted, respected, and able to be their best. A bully free school is a Golden Rule School—where everyone treats others the way they want to be treated.

We hope that you find this book useful in your effort to promote anti-bullying messages and improve the climate at your school. We'd enjoy hearing about any experiences you have with the book—or creative ideas you and your students come up with while working together. Also feel free to send photographs of finished displays. With your permission, our publisher may include them on the company Web site (www.freespirit.com) to share ideas with other schools. You may contact us in care of our publisher:

Allan and Linda Beane
c/o Free Spirit Publishing
217 Fifth Avenue North, Suite 200
Minneapolis, MN 55401-1299
help4kids@freespirit.com

Bully Free Bulletin Boards, Posters, and Banners is organized to offer you opportunities to have meaningful and sustained discussion with students about bullying, its effects, and ways it can be prevented. Assembling displays on your own is okay—getting the bully free message out in your school can help significantly. A primary focus of this book, though, is involving students in the creation of displays while maintaining dialog with them about important anti-bullying concepts. When students are engaged and enjoying themselves in creating displays, they're more apt to remember key ideas about bullying—some of which they themselves bring to the discussion.

Because you know your students' and classroom needs better than anyone, we've structured this book so that you can use it in any way that works best for you. Display directions are meant to guide you and are not intended as strict rules to follow. Variations are offered along the way—some of which you'll want to try, others you won't. In short, feel free to make any alterations to displays that you see fit.

The bulletin boards portion of the book begins on page 7. Bulletin boards are organized by sophistication—elementary-level displays appear first and those for middle school students follow (beginning on page 59).

Each bulletin board idea makes up two pages:

The left-hand page features an illustration of what the display will look like when completed, as well as directions for creating the bulletin board. It's also here that you'll find "Variation" ideas. These are often suggestions for involving students in different ways, using different materials, or tying bulletin boards to the seasons or important events on the school calendar. Finally, each page includes a "What to Talk About" section—a listing of several topics and questions to discuss with students as you work together to make the bulletin boards.

The right-hand page features art templates you can use to create the bulletin board. The templates can be enlarged using an overhead projector by following these steps:

1. Lay the book down flat.

2. Place a clear overhead sheet on top of the art template and trace the pattern.

3. Choose paper of a kind and size that's appropriate for your display and tape it to a wall.

4. Place the overhead sheet on the overhead machine and project the form onto the paper. (Move the projector nearer to or farther from the wall—as necessary—to shrink or enlarge the image.)

5. Trace the image on the paper.

You can also use a copy machine to enlarge templates. Simply place the art face down on the window and use the machine's controls to increase the image's size to meet your needs.

In addition to the art accompanying the bulletin boards, you'll find more templates on pages 134–135 that can be enlarged and copied for use on displays. Sometimes the right-hand page will only have some of the templates a bulletin board incorporates. In such cases, directions will point you to these additional templates.

The alphabets that you can use for bulletin board titles are found on pages 130–133. You can create the titles for boards using an overhead projector or copy machine by enlarging and tracing letters in the same way you do art templates.

Bulletin board themes can also be banners. (See pages 118–127.) Or bulletin boards can be downsized and created in the form of posters. (For examples, see pages 110–117.) Rather than use bulletin board paper, simply use tag board, construction paper, or another format that meets your needs for a base and appropriately size the lettering and art templates.

How you use the bulletin boards is up to you. You may wish to closely follow the described plans, or choose to customize and enhance the displays to meet your needs and those of your students. You might, for example, wish to add your school's name or mascot to the displays you create. Or, rather than use only paper for displays, you may wish to include photographs, magazine clippings, or three-dimensional materials (like fabric, string, or yarn). Students may have even more ideas for customizing the displays and livening things up. A great way to engage middle school students is to involve the student council, advisories, and other student leader groups in organizing contests for creating displays for hallways, doors, and classrooms around specific themes or based on school events. Think of this book as a springboard to letting your and students' creativity come out!

Most important in creating displays is engaging students and getting them thinking about bullying and its effects on the school climate. The "What to Talk About" sections feature discussion questions you can use with students. Sometimes these questions address what should be done in specific bullying situations. Other times, they offer students opportunities to talk about themselves in positive ways—about how they are unique, about the kind actions they perform for others, and other qualities they have that can boost self-esteem and help to build community. Other questions focus on bullying that students have seen or experienced themselves. Advise students who share bullying stories to follow the "no names" rule—that is, to keep the names of involved students out of the discussion. During your discussions, you can reference examples of bully free actions, bully free qualities, and feelings. Lists of these are located on pages 136–138. Specific page numbers are referenced in the "What to Talk About" sections when lists might be particularly helpful.

Maintaining a continual dialog on anti-bullying concepts as you put displays together allows you to reinforce them and help students remember them. This dialog is also an opportunity to get student feedback on how you and other staff can better address bullying.

Beyond creating displays with students, you can also take opportunities in class or at other times with the group to talk about bullying—or incorporate anti-bullying concepts into content areas. You might ask students to read and report on books that deal with bullying, friendship, and conflict resolution. Discuss the books in class, or have students write original stories featuring characters from the reading. With older students, civics lessons often feature prominent peacemakers and discussions of social issues related to respect, individual rights, and diversity.

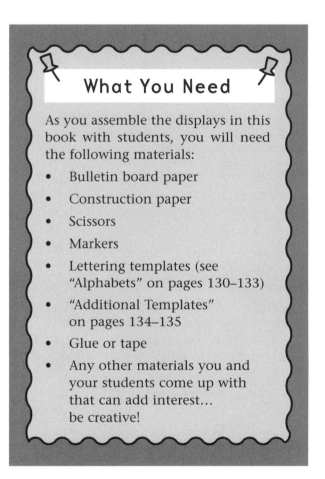

What You Need

As you assemble the displays in this book with students, you will need the following materials:

- Bulletin board paper
- Construction paper
- Scissors
- Markers
- Lettering templates (see "Alphabets" on pages 130–133)
- "Additional Templates" on pages 134–135
- Glue or tape
- Any other materials you and your students come up with that can add interest... be creative!

Definition

Bullying is a form of overt and aggressive behavior that is intentional, hurtful, and repeated. With bullying, there is an imbalance of strength; bullied children are harassed, taunted, rejected, and assaulted by one or more individuals. People who bully often want to have power over others.

Myths About Bullying

- **Bullying is just teasing.** Teasing happens between people who view each other as equals. With bullying, there is an imbalance of power. While teasing can be fun, bullying always hurts the person who is bullied.

- **Some people deserve to be bullied.** No one ever deserves to be bullied or "asks for it." Everyone deserves to feel safe and respected at school.

- **People who complain about bullying are babies.** People who complain about bullying are standing up for themselves and trying to get the respect they deserve.

- **Only boys bully.** Both boys and girls bully others.

- **Bullying is a normal part of growing up.** Getting teased, picked on, pushed around, threatened, harassed, insulted, hurt, and abused is not normal—it's wrong, and it's important to do something to stop it.

- **People who bully will stop the behavior if you ignore them.** Some people who bully only get more upset when ignored. They want their behavior to get attention.

- **All people who bully have low self-esteem—that's why they pick on others.** Some people who bully have high self-esteem. They think they are better than others.

- **It's tattling to tell an adult when you're bullied.** It's smart to tell someone who can do something to help stop the bullying. It's not tattling, it's reporting.

- **The best way to deal with someone who bullies is by fighting or trying to get even.** If you fight or tease someone who is bullying, the person may only get angry and try to hurt you even worse.

- **People who are bullied will get over it.** Bullying hurts for a long time and causes some children to drop out of school. Others become lonely, sad, or depressed. As a result of bullying, some kids have committed suicide or struck out violently at school.

Kinds of Bullying

- **Physical:** hitting, slapping, pushing, pinching, tripping, and kicking

- **Verbal:** teasing, name-calling, using sexist, racist, or bigoted remarks, and making threats

- **Relational:** intimidation, coercion, spreading rumors or lies—including through email or phone text messaging—and exclusion

Appropriate Student Responses to Bullying

- **Report it.** Bullying should always be reported—both by students who are bullied and those who witness bullying. Teachers, parents, and other adults cannot help if they do not know a bullying situation is going on.

- **If it is safe, stand up to bullying.** Students can say, "Leave me alone" or "Stop bullying now" in a clear, strong voice. People who bully often target others who do not seem confident.

- **Try to stay around others.** People who bully often pick on kids who are alone.

- **Avoid the person who is bullying.** Whenever it is possible, stay away from people who bully others.

- **If a situation is dangerous, get away as quickly as possible.** Getting out of the situation is a good way to stay safe.

- **Befriend those who have been bullied.** People who are bullied often feel lonely and isolated.

- **When a person is not bullying, try to be friendly.** People who bully often want to be liked by others but do not know positive ways to show it.

Inappropriate Student Responses to Bullying

- **Fighting back or trying to get even.** More fighting or conflict can only make a situation worse.

- **Joining in bullying.** Bullying is wrong and should be stopped.

- **Staying quiet about the bullying.** Speaking out against bullying makes school safer for everyone.

Appropriate Educator Responses to Bullying

If you witness bullying, take immediate action:

- When bullying is physical, instruct the student to stop the hurtful action immediately and to move away from the person who is being bullied. Clearly communicate that the behavior is not acceptable.

- When bullying is verbal, instruct the student to stop using unacceptable language. Clearly communicate that the language is not appropriate.

- When bullying is relational, instruct the student to stop the behavior immediately. Clearly communicate that everyone is welcome and accepted at school.

If you hear about bullying, investigate:

- Closely observe the students—both the student who bullied and the person who was bullied—together and apart.

- Speak separately to both students, trying to determine how truthful their responses are.

- Talk with any students that may have witnessed the bullying. The student you heard about the incident from and friends of those involved in the bullying incident are good places to start.

- Talk with other school personnel that frequently interact with the students involved.

Follow up on all bullying incidents:

- Keep a record of all conversations and steps taken. Clearly establish and document what's happened, when and where it occurred, and who was involved.

- Talk with the student who bullied and the person who was bullied separately after the incident occurs.

- Interview witnesses of the bullying individually.

- Talk with other school faculty—including administration—about the bullying incident and your conversations with the students involved.

- Contact the parents of involved students. Inform them of the incident and arrange to meet with them separately.

- Maintain contact with school faculty and parents until the situation is clearly resolved.

- Consult your school or district's policies regarding bullying incidents.

Rules for a Bully Free Classroom

1. Bullying is not allowed in our classroom (or anywhere else in the school).

2. We don't tease, call names, or put people down.

3. We don't hit, shove, kick, or punch.

4. If we see someone being bullied, we speak up and stop it (if we can) or go for help right away.

5. When we do things as a group, we make sure that everyone is included and no one is left out.

6. We make new students feel welcome.

7. We listen to each other's opinions.

8. We treat each other with kindness and respect.

9. We respect each other's property. (School property, too.)

10. We look for the good in others and value differences.

For More Information on Bullying

The Bully Free Classroom™: Over 100 Tips and Strategies for Teachers K–8 (Updated Edition) by Allan L. Beane, Ph.D. (Minneapolis: Free Spirit Publishing, 2005). Prevention and intervention strategies teachers can start using immediately in the classroom—with students who bully, those who are bullied, and bystanders.

Bully Free Systems (www.bullyfree.com). The mission of this company is to help schools create bully free environments where the Golden Rule is observed by all students and staff. Visit the site for resources and speaking and training opportunities.

The Bully, the Bullied, and the Bystander: From Preschool to High School—How Parents and Teachers Can Break the Cycle of Violence by Barbara Coloroso (New York: HarperCollins, 2003). For any adult working with children, this book offers strategies for empowering students against mistreatment.

Center for the Prevention of School Violence (www.ncdjjdp.org/cpsv). This organization distributes current research on school violence and offers educators tools they can use to try and stop it. Log on to the Web site to learn about ways to promote a safer learning environment at your school.

National School Safety Center (www.nssc1.org). This organization works toward the prevention of school crime and violence worldwide. It offers resources and training services to schools and serves to identify and promote best practices and programs.

Office of Safe and Drug-Free Schools (www.ed.gov/offices/oese/sdfs). This is the office of the U.S. Department of Education responsible for ensuring America's schools are healthy and nurturing learning environments. The Web site features a wealth of information, including an action plan for decreasing instances of bullying and school violence.

----------ELEMENTARY SCHOOL----------
DISPLAYS

Treat Others the Way You Want to Be Treated

You can use this display to help students understand the Golden Rule. Treating others as we'd like to be treated allows everyone at school to get along and feel accepted.

WHAT TO DO

1. Cover the board with bulletin board paper.

2. Enlarge, copy, and cut out the letters for the display title from construction paper and mount them on the board.

3. Ask students to choose a sheet of construction paper. As needed, help children trace and cut out a figure. (For additional figures and accessories, see pages 134–135.) Have students use markers to decorate their figures, adding faces, clothing, and other features. You may also wish to have students write their names on their figures.

4. Help students mount their figures on the board.

WHAT TO TALK ABOUT

As you work on this display with students, talk about the Golden Rule and how it helps everyone feel safe and accepted at school. We all want to be treated with kindness and respect, and we can treat others in the same way. When we follow the Golden Rule, our words and actions are positive—they make others feel respected, supported, and confident. We don't use negative words and actions; negative words and actions can hurt others and make them feel upset, afraid, or sad. Speaking to and treating others in positive ways helps us get along, feel liked by others, and have fun at school. During your discussion of the Golden Rule, you can use questions like the following:

1. "Treat others the way you want to be treated" is the Golden Rule. What are some words we can use and actions we can show at school to follow the Golden Rule? (For examples, see "Bully Free Actions" on page 136.)

2. How do you feel when people are kind and respectful to you? How do you feel when people act mean or nasty? (For examples of emotions, see "Feelings" on page 138.)

3. Why is it important to follow the Golden Rule? How does it make school a better place for everyone to learn?

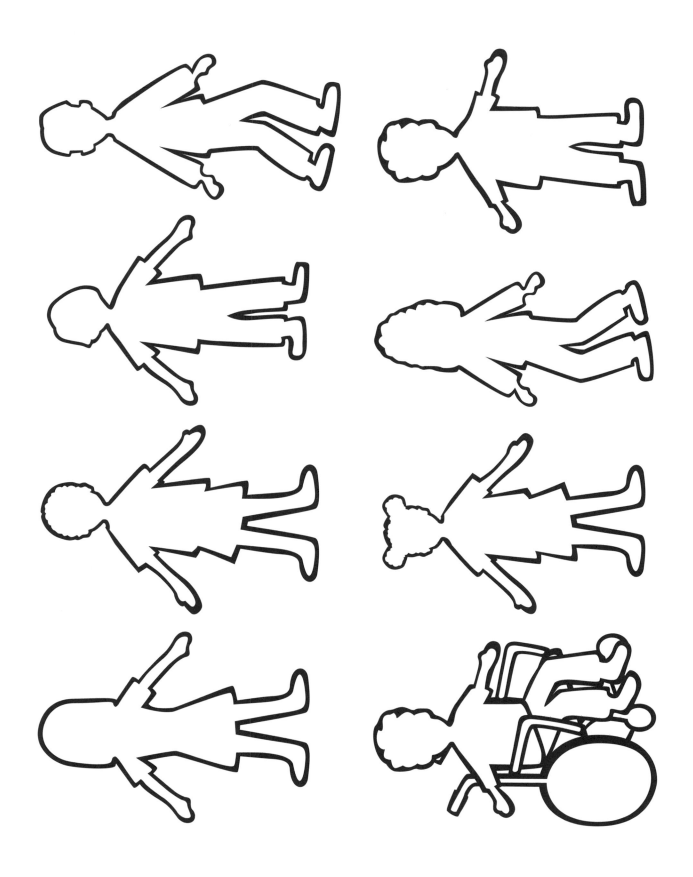

You can use this display to reinforce that all students deserve to feel accepted and respected at school—including those children who are new to the classroom or often teased or left out.

WHAT TO DO

1. Cover the board with bulletin board paper.

2. Enlarge, copy, and cut out the letters for the display title from construction paper and mount them on the board.

3. Enlarge, copy, and cut out the school and mount it on the board.

4. Invite students to select a sheet of construction paper. Help children as needed to trace and cut out a figure. (Additional figure templates can be found throughout this book and on pages 134–135.) Ask students to use markers to decorate their figures by adding faces, clothing, and their names. If you wish, give children additional construction paper and let them draw and cut out accessories like backpacks and playground equipment to add to the display.

5. Help students mount their figures on the board.

Variation: Rather than have each student cut out and customize a figure, you may wish to mount students' photographs on the board. Help children to place photographs on the board surrounding the school pattern, and write students' names underneath them. You may ask students to bring photos from home or snap pictures of children in the classroom.

WHAT TO TALK ABOUT

As you help students mount their figures (or photographs) on the board, discuss why it's important to welcome and respect all students at school. You can talk about how people feel good about themselves when they're accepted; they feel liked and are able achieve their best in the classroom. Talk about how it feels to be left out—children may feel sad, lonely, and like they don't belong with the group. Discuss things students can do to make others feel welcome, like sit with them at lunch, ask them to play on the playground, or help them with a problem. (For more ideas, see "Bully Free Actions" on page 136.) During this discussion, you can use questions like the following:

1. Why is it important for everyone to feel welcome at school?

2. Have you ever felt nervous or afraid on the first day in a new class or school? What happened?

3. What can we do to make everyone feel welcome in our classroom?

You can use this display to talk about how being friendly to others makes school a more pleasant place to learn.

WHAT TO DO _ _ _ _ _ _ _ _ _ _ _ _ _

1. Cover the board with bulletin board paper.

2. Enlarge, copy, and cut out the letters for the display title from construction paper and mount them on the board.

3. Enlarge, copy, and cut out the flowers and mount them on the board.

4. Ask children to select a piece of construction paper. As necessary, help students to trace and cut out a bee for the display. Have children use markers to customize their bees by adding decorations and one friendly action.

5. Help students mount their bees on the board.

Variation: Rather than cut out flowers from construction paper, use cloth or plastic flowers to give the display a three-dimensional quality. Cloth and plastic flowers can often be found inexpensively priced at discount stores.

WHAT TO TALK ABOUT _ _ _ _ _ _ _ _

As you assemble this display with students, talk about the many ways people can be friendly. For example, students can smile and say hello, listen when others speak, and share their things. These are all friendly actions—ways to show that you respect and care for others. (For more friendly actions, see "Bully Free Actions" on page 136.) As you help students add their bees to the display, talk about how the positive actions they've chosen to write down make the classroom a more pleasant place. Throughout this discussion, you can use questions like the following:

1. What friendly action did you write on your bee? What happens when you smile and say hello (listen to others, share your things)? How do you feel?

2. How do you feel when people are friendly to you? How do you feel when people are not friendly? (For examples of emotions, see "Feelings" on page 138.)

3. How does being friendly help us get along and feel supported at school?

This display can be used to broadly discuss bullying—and to get students thinking about positive actions they can show in the classroom.

WHAT TO DO

1. Cover the board with bulletin board paper.

2. Enlarge, copy, and cut out the letters for the display title from construction paper and mount them on the board.

3. Invite students to choose a sheet of construction paper. Help children as needed to trace and cut out their fish. Ask students to customize their fish by adding their names, decorations, and one positive action they show to stay bully free.

4. Help students mount their fish on the board.

WHAT TO TALK ABOUT

As you assemble this display with students, talk about bullying and its negative effects on the school environment. (You may wish to reference "Bullying Basics" on pages 4–6.) When students are ready to mount their fish on the board, ask them for ways they can act to help make the classroom a safe and pleasant place to learn—a bully free classroom. For example, inviting someone to join in a game makes a person feel welcome. Listening to others helps you understand how they feel; it lets you talk

out problems instead of fighting about them. Inviting someone to join in and listening are kind, helpful ways to act—they are positive actions that help us get along together in the classroom. (For other positive actions, see "Bully Free Actions" on page 136.) Have children use markers to write positive actions on their fish. Talk about how each positive action makes the classroom a safer and better place. You can relate student behavior to that of fish. Fish swim in schools for protection; they stay together so that they can be safe from predators. Sticking together can also help students stay safe when they are kind to and watch out for one another. Throughout this discussion, you can use questions like the following:

1. What positive actions are important to show in our classroom? How do they help us to get along and stay safe?

2. How do you feel when someone smiles at you (invites you to join, listens to you)? (For examples of emotions, see "Feelings" on page 138.)

3. Do you remember a time when someone acted unfriendly or mean? What happened? How did you feel?

This display can be used to talk about appropriate and inappropriate actions for the classroom.

WHAT TO DO _ _ _ _ _ _ _ _ _ _ _

1. Cover the board with bulletin board paper.

2. Enlarge, copy, and cut out the letters for the display title from construction paper and mount them on the board.

3. Enlarge, copy, and cut out the train engine. Mount it on the board.

4. Ask students to select a sheet of construction paper. As needed, help children trace and cut out train cars. Students may customize their train cars by adding decorations, their names, and one positive action they do to keep behavior "on track" at school.

5. Help students mount their train cars on the board. Use a marker to connect the train cars with each other.

Variation: Use three-dimensional objects to make this display come to life. Large buttons glued to the train engine and cars can serve as wheels. You may use yarn—rather than a marker—to connect the engine and the train cars. Gluing a few pulled-apart cotton balls above the smoke stack of the engine can create the effect of puffs of smoke.

WHAT TO TALK ABOUT _ _ _ _ _ _ _ _ _

As you put together this display with students, talk about what it means to stay "on track." For example, speaking kindly at an appropriate level of voice lets everyone feel respected. Cooperating with others during classroom activities lets everyone get work done and feel proud of what they have done. (For other positive actions, see "Bully Free Actions" on page 136.) Use the metaphor of a train running along a track to discuss appropriate classroom behavior. When one car goes off of the track, all of the other cars are affected and the train cannot move. At school, one person showing inappropriate behavior affects the entire class. When children make loud or mean remarks during class, for example, feelings are hurt, the lesson is disrupted, and others may fear that they will also be teased. Throughout this discussion, you can use questions like the following:

1. What does it mean to keep behavior "on track" at school?

2. What are some "on track" behaviors for the classroom? What are some "off track" behaviors?

3. Why is it important for everyone in the group to keep behavior "on track"?

You can use this display to help students understand that their positive actions not only let them be their best, but also bring out the best in others.

WHAT TO DO _ _ _ _ _ _ _ _ _ _ _ _ _ _ _ _

1. Cover the board with bulletin board paper.

2. Enlarge, copy, and cut out the letters for the display title from construction paper and mount them on the board.

3. Enlarge, copy, and cut out candle template from construction paper and mount it on the board.

4. Ask students to choose a sheet of construction paper. As needed, help children trace and cut out a candle ray. Have students use markers to customize their candle rays by adding decorations and one positive action they show to "let their light shine."

5. Help students mount candle rays on the board.

WHAT TO TALK ABOUT _ _ _ _ _ _ _ _ _

As you assemble this display with students, talk about how being kind and respectful to others helps them to act in the same way toward us.

For example, when we use kind and polite words, others feel safe and respected; they can use the same positive words because they know that we accept and value them. When we cooperate with others, we can work together to create cool projects—like this display! (For more positive actions, see "Bully Free Actions" on page 136.) As students mount their candle rays on the board, discuss in detail each of the positive actions they have written. Throughout your discussion, you can use questions like the following:

1. How does playing fairly (using kind and polite words, cooperating with others) let your light shine?

2. How do you feel when you play fairly (use kind and polite words, cooperate with others)? How can your best actions bring out the best in others?

3. How does playing fairly (using kind and polite words, cooperating with others) make our classroom a better place for everyone to learn?

What I Like About You

You can use this display to talk about the importance of using words in positive ways. It's also a great opportunity to affirm students by sharing with them the qualities that you admire in them.

WHAT TO DO

1. Cover the board with bulletin board paper.

2. Enlarge, copy, and cut out the letters for the display title from construction paper and mount them on the board.

3. Invite students to select a sheet of construction paper. As needed, help children trace and cut out ice cream cones. Have students use markers to write their names on the cones.

4. On each student's ice cream cone, write a positive quality or phrase that you believe describes him or her.

5. Help students mount ice cream cones on the board.

WHAT TO TALK ABOUT

As you work with students on this display, talk about how we use words. When we use mean words ("You're dumb. I don't like you.") we hurt others' feelings. Instead, we should try to use words in kind ways. Words can be used to greet others. ("Hi!" "How are you?" "It's nice to see you.") Words can be used to cooperate and get along. ("Let's play together." "We can take turns.") They can be used to talk about how we feel. ("I'm excited to play." "I'm worried about the spelling test.") And to be polite. ("Can I please have a cookie?" "Thanks!") One other very nice way to use words is to give compliments. Compliments make others feel good. We can compliment people on talents, positive qualities, or unique things about them. When you help students mount their ice cream cones on the board, talk about what you have written on their cones. Invite children to add their thoughts. As you discuss using kind words, you can use questions like the following:

1. I think Joe (Kwame, Cynthia) is very thoughtful (helpful, a great speller). Do you agree?

2. What are some other good qualities about Joe (Kwame, Cynthia)?

3. How do you feel when you compliment others? (For examples of emotions, see "Feelings" on page 138.)

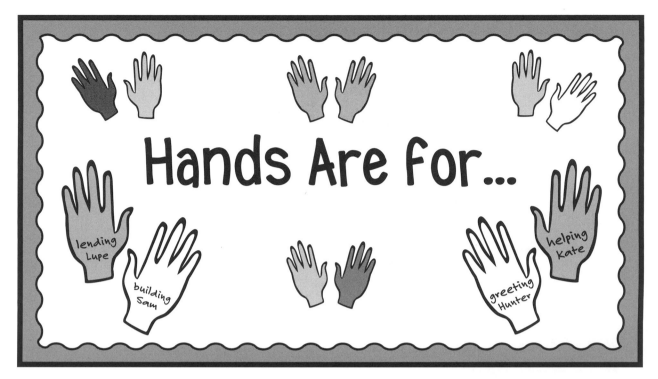

You can use this display to talk with students about positive actions they perform with their hands.

WHAT TO DO

1. Cover the board with bulletin board paper.

2. Enlarge, copy, and cut out the letters for the display title from construction paper and mount them on the board.

3. Ask students to choose a piece of construction paper. Help children as needed to trace and cut out outlines of one of their hands. (An alternative is to use the hand templates at right.) Invite students to customize their hands by adding decorations, their names, and one positive action they perform with their hands.

4. Help students mount the hand patterns on the board.

Variation: Ask students to cut out scenes from magazines of helpful actions being performed with hands. Have students glue scenes to their hand outlines before you help to mount them on the display.

WHAT TO TALK ABOUT

As you put together this display with students, talk about both the negative and positive actions that hands can do. When we do unkind things with our hands (push, pinch, or take others' things) people can be hurt and feel bad. When we perform positive actions (wave hello, write someone a nice note, or give a high five) others feel good. (For more ideas, see "Bully Free Actions" on page 136.) Talk about how each positive action makes the learning environment better for everyone. (If you've chosen to use scenes from magazines, talk about the kind action being performed in the picture.) You can use questions like the following:

1. What are some unkind things that people do with their hands? What are some kind things hands can do?

2. How have you used your hands to help others? How did you feel? How do you feel when others help you? (For examples of emotions, see "Feelings" on page 138.)

3. How does using our hands in positive ways make the classroom a better place to learn?

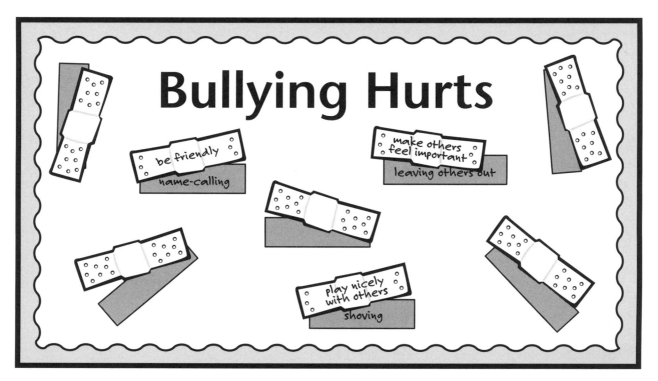

You can use this board to discuss the harmful effects of bullying—and to pose positive alternatives to bullying behaviors.

WHAT TO DO

1. Cover the board with bulletin board paper.

2. Enlarge, copy, and cut out the letters for the display title from construction paper and mount them on the board.

3. Enlarge, copy, and cut out rectangle patterns. Ask the class for examples of bullying behaviors and write them on the rectangles. Mount the rectangles on the board.

4. Enlarge, copy, and cut out the bandages. Ask students for examples of positive actions they can show. Write the positive actions on the bandages.

5. Help students mount the bandages on the board so that they partially cover up the bullying behaviors on the rectangles.

WHAT TO TALK ABOUT

As you put together this display with students, discuss what bullying behaviors are and how they hurt others. For example, calling others names or saying mean things can make them feel bad and like they don't belong at school.

Pinching and hitting hurt and others. (You may reference "Bullying Basics" on pages 4–6 for more examples of bullying behaviors.) Discuss how the positive alternatives on the bandages make others feel. For example, instead of teasing others, we can use kind words to make people feel welcome. Instead of hitting or pinching, we can use our hands to help others. As you discuss bullying behaviors and positive alternatives, you can use questions like the following:

1. Why is it wrong to shove (call others names, say mean things, hit, pinch)? How do you feel when people do this to you? (For examples of emotions, see "Feelings" on page 138.)

2. Why is it good to play nicely (say kind words, help others)? How do you feel when people are kind to you?

3. What kind of bullying hurts the most? Teasing? Hitting? Leaving others out? (Answers will likely vary. Talk about why—everyone has unique feelings—and use that as a reason to show that no bullying behavior is acceptable.)

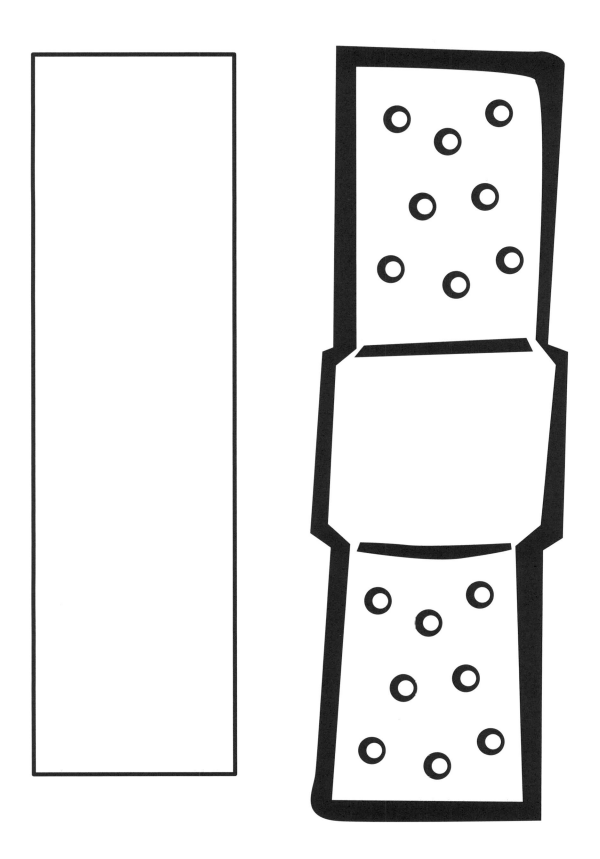

BULLY FREE TREE

You can use this display to talk about how we are all different from each other in certain ways, but that we can get along and celebrate each other.

WHAT TO DO _ _ _ _ _ _ _ _ _ _ _ _ _ _

1. Cover the board with bulletin board paper.

2. Enlarge, copy, and cut out the letters for the display title from construction paper and mount them on the board.

3. Enlarge, copy, and cut out the tree pattern from construction paper. Mount it on the board.

4. Ask students to select a piece of construction paper. Help children as needed to trace and cut out leaves. Have students use markers to decorate their leaves and add their names.

5. Help students to mount their leaves on the board.

Variation: This bulletin board works well as either a spring or fall display. The color of leaves can be varied to reflect the season. For a spring display, leaves can be placed amidst the tree's branches. For a fall display, leaves can be placed falling to the ground at the base of the tree.

WHAT TO TALK ABOUT _ _ _ _ _ _ _ _ _

As you work on this display, talk about the many ways in which we're different. We have different physical features (height, weight, hair, eyes, and skin). We also have different families, interests, beliefs, and things we are good at. Still, we are more alike than we're different. We all have feelings, like to play, want to learn, and deserve to be treated well. Use a tree and its leaves as a metaphor for the classroom; leaves look a lot alike but each one is different in small ways—in size, shape, and color. Just like all of the leaves—including their differences—add to the beauty and health of a tree, everyone in the classroom makes it a more fun and interesting place; everyone learns new things and works together to complete projects. Throughout your discussion, you can use questions like the following:

1. What are some ways that we are different from each other? How are we all alike?

2. Why is it important to accept and show respect for people who are different from us?

3. How do our differences make class more interesting and fun? What would life be like if we were all exactly the same?

Like Snowflakes, We're Unique!

Use this display to boost students' self-esteem by helping them realize they have special gifts that they share with the group. At the same time, you can promote acceptance.

WHAT TO DO _ _ _ _ _ _ _ _ _ _ _ _ _

1. Cover the board with bulletin board paper.

2. Enlarge, copy, and cut out the letters for the display title from construction paper and mount them on the board.

3. Enlarge, copy, and cut out the snowperson pattern from construction paper. Mount it on the board.

4. Invite students to create their own snow-flakes from construction paper. (If you are not familiar with how to create snow-flakes, visit www.snowflakes.com to find a variety of patterns for different skill levels. Another alternative is to use the snow-flakes at right.) Have students use markers to customize snowflakes by adding decorations, their names, and one quality that makes them unique.

5. Help students mount their snowflakes on the board.

WHAT TO TALK ABOUT _ _ _ _ _ _ _ _ _

When you work on this display with students, talk about how—just like snowflakes—no two people are the same. Our unique qualities make us individuals, and should make us proud. While we all have things that make us unique— physical qualities, personality traits, interests, and talents—we are alike in other ways and want many of the same things. As you help students mount their snowflakes on the board, affirm children by praising the qualities that they have chosen to write down. Ask others in the group to comment on qualities. Use the metaphor that even though every snowflake has its own signature cut, all snowflakes are more alike than they are different. (Plus, all snowflakes can be rolled up and together into a snowperson!) For your discussion, you can use questions like the following:

1. What unique quality or talent did you write on your snowflake?

2. I think it's great that (Sara can draw so well, Torii helps others with math, Kelsey is kind). What do you think?

3. How do our unique talents and quali-ties make class a good place to learn new things?

You can use this display to talk about positive, bully free behaviors that let students shine—like stars—and to give students a refresher course on our solar system!

WHAT TO DO _ _ _ _ _ _ _ _ _ _ _ _ _ _

1. Cover the board with bulletin board paper.

2. Enlarge, copy, and cut out the letters for the display title from construction paper and mount them on the board.

3. Enlarge, copy, and cut out the sun and planets. Use differently sized and colored circle patterns to reflect the planets in our solar system. Mount the sun and planets on the display. Use a marker to draw planets' orbits around the sun.

4. Invite students to choose a sheet of construction paper. As needed, help children trace and cut out stars. Have students use markers to decorate their stars with their names and positive, bully free actions.

5. Help students to mount their stars on the board.

WHAT TO TALK ABOUT _ _ _ _ _ _ _ _ _

As you assemble this bulletin board with students, talk about the differences between negative and positive behaviors. Negative actions can hurt others, make them feel bad, and escalate conflicts. Positive actions allow us to show respect for and get along with others—they let us "shine" in the classroom. Some examples are following directions, asking others to join in, taking turns, and talking out problems. (For more examples of positive actions, see "Bully Free Actions" on page 136.) Discuss the positive actions students wrote down, talking about how they help a classroom to be bully free. You can use questions like the following:

1. What positive action did you write on your star?

2. How does the action you wrote make the classroom a safer place to learn?

3. What does it mean to "be a star" or to "shine"? How do positive actions let us shine?

Use this display to discuss different forms of playground bullying and appropriate student responses to it.

WHAT TO DO

1. Cover the board with bulletin board paper.

2. Enlarge, copy, and cut out the letters for the display title from construction paper and mount them on the board.

3. Enlarge, copy, and cut out the playground equipment and game squares. Mount them on the board.

4. Invite students to choose a sheet of construction paper. As needed, help children trace and cut out figures. (See figure templates throughout this book and on pages 134–135.) Have students use markers to decorate their figures, adding faces, clothing, and their names.

5. Help students mount their figures on the board.

Variation: This bulletin board can be also used as a game. Students' figures can be placed at the start and moved forward when they show positive, bully free actions on the playground over the course of a week, month, or year. Work to reward all students so that the whole group feels involved. When someone gets to the end, the game begins again. Throughout the game, encourage students to catch each other "being good" and to report it.

WHAT TO TALK ABOUT

As you assemble this bulletin board with students, talk about bullying that happens on the playground. Emphasize that school breaks are times for everyone to have fun, and that it's important to treat others well. Showing respect, inviting others to join in, sharing, and taking turns are all ways to help everyone get along on the playground—and to stay bully free. Send a clear message that all bullying that does occur should be reported immediately. In your discussion with students, you can use questions like the following:

1. What kinds of bullying happen on the playground?

2. Have you ever been bullied on the playground? What happened? How did you feel?

3. What are some things we can do to stop bullying from happening on the playground? How does respecting others (including others, sharing, taking turns) on the playground make it a better place for everyone to play?

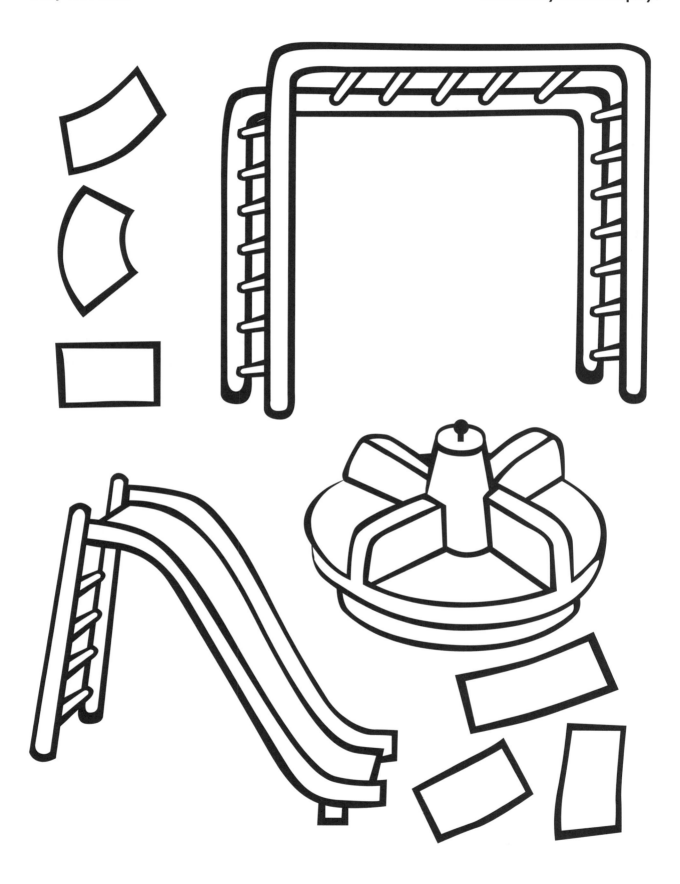

This board can be used to emphasize the importance of peaceful actions in the classroom.

WHAT TO DO _ _ _ _ _ _ _ _ _ _ _ _ _ _ _

1. Cover the board with bulletin board paper.

2. Work with students to enlarge, copy, and cut out the letters for the display title from construction paper and mount them on the board.

3. Help students to enlarge, copy, and cut out the figures and mount them on the board. Students can use markers to decorate figures by adding facial features and clothing.

WHAT TO TALK ABOUT _ _ _ _ _ _ _ _ _

As you assemble this display with students, talk about what peace is. When we are peaceful, we are friendly, considerate, and gentle. When we have disagreements with others, we do not hit, push, kick, or use other forms of violence. Instead, we talk about how we feel and listen to the other person's side. In the classroom, being

peaceful includes saying please, thank you, and other polite words, following the rules, and speaking at an appropriate level of voice. As you talk with students, use a marker to write the peaceful actions you come up with together on the display. (For more peaceful actions, see "Bully Free Actions" on page 136.) Throughout this discussion, you may wish to reference well-known peacemakers—like Martin Luther King Jr., Elie Wiesel, and His Holiness the Dalai Lama of Tibet. You can use questions like the following:

1. What is peace? Why is peace important in the classroom?

2. What are some peaceful actions we can show at school?

3. What can happen when people are not peaceful?

Our School Is a Place Where...

we play fairly

we use kind greetings

we give compliments

Jack

Macy

Ruth

Dani

Tong

we ask permission to use others' things

we show others respect

we stand up for others

You can use this display to discuss the concept of "community" and to promote a caring and supportive school.

WHAT TO DO

1. Cover the board with bulletin board paper.

2. Enlarge, copy, and cut out the letters for the display title from construction paper and mount them on the board.

3. Invite students to choose a sheet of construction paper. Help children as needed to trace and cut out figures. (Additional figure templates can be found throughout this book and on pages 134–135.) Ask students to use markers to add clothing, physical features, and their names to their figures.

4. Help students mount the figures on the board.

Variation: Customize this display for your setting by adding your school logo or mascot. You can also alter the bulletin board title to include the name of your school (for example, "Turner Elementary School Is a Place Where...").

WHAT TO TALK ABOUT

As you work with students on this display, talk about the benefits of a school where students care for and support each other—everyone feels safe and accepted, and it's easier for children to learn. When students are ready to mount their figures on the board, ask individually for positive actions that promote community at school. You can help students if they have trouble coming up with positive actions. For example, we can use kind greetings, congratulate and compliment each other, solve problems peacefully, and treat each other the way we'd like to be treated. (For more positive actions that promote community, see "Bully Free Actions" on page 136.) Use markers to write positive actions on the board as students mount their figures on the display. You can use questions like the following:

1. Why is it important to have a school where students care for and support each other?

2. What can happen when people do not feel safe and cared for at school?

3. What can we do to help everyone feel secure, confident, and happy at school?

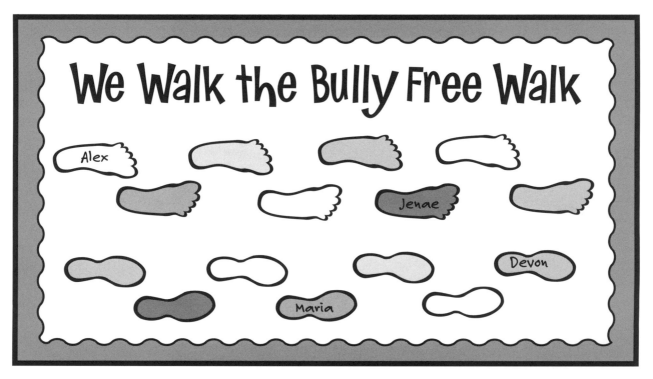

This display can be used to broadly discuss bullying, as well as the steps that should be taken when it occurs.

WHAT TO DO _ _ _ _ _ _ _ _ _ _ _ _ _ _ _ _ _

1. Cover the board with bulletin board paper.

2. Enlarge, copy, and cut out the letters for the display title from construction paper and mount them on the board.

3. Invite students to choose a sheet of construction paper. As needed, help children trace and cut out one of their footprints. (An alternative is to use the footprint templates at right.) Have students use markers to decorate and add their names to their footprints.

4. Help students mount footprints on the board.

WHAT TO TALK ABOUT _ _ _ _ _ _ _ _ _

As you put together this display with students, talk about what bullying is, how it hurts people, and what should be done when it occurs. (See "Bullying Basics" on pages 4–6 for information.) When students are ready to mount their footprints on the board, ask them to name one positive action they can do to help make the classroom a safe and respectful environment—a bully free classroom. For example, using polite and kind words, sharing, and helping others feel accepted and respected. (See "Bully Free Actions" on page 136 for more examples of positive actions.) Discuss each of the actions that students bring up, talking about how each can make children feel safe and secure at school. You can use questions like the following:

1. Have you ever been bullied? What happened? How did you feel? (For examples of emotions, see "Feelings" on page 138.)

2. How do you feel when people cooperate (use kind words, share, help you with something)?

3. How does cooperating (using polite words, sharing, helping others) make school better for all of us?

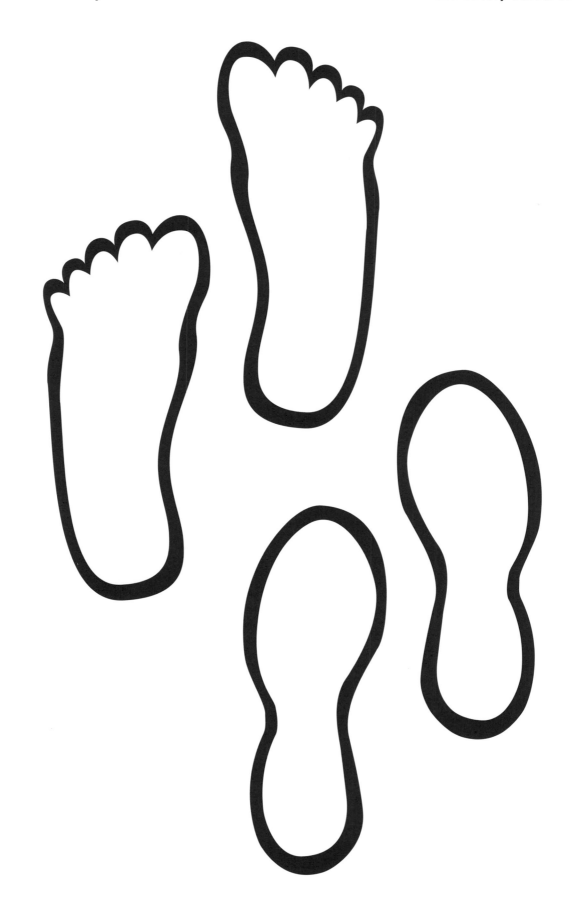

OUR SCHOOL IS A SAFE BULLY FREE HARBOR

This display can be used to explore what it means to feel safe—both physically and emotionally—and to discuss how bullying is harmful to the school environment.

WHAT TO DO

1. Cover the board with bulletin board paper.

2. Work with students to enlarge, copy, and cut out the letters for the display title from construction paper and mount them on the board.

3. Help children to enlarge, copy, and cut out the ship, sun, and cloud patterns. Mount them on the board.

Variation: Ask a few students to work on creating figures for the display (as shown above). Figure templates can be found throughout this book and on pages 134–135. Students may also use markers to add gulls or other wildlife.

WHAT TO TALK ABOUT

As you put together this display with students, discuss what it means to feel safe. When people feel safe they are in a place or situation where they don't worry about being hurt—they know others will not hit, kick, name call, put down, or do other mean or violent things. When children feel safe, they feel secure, trusting, comfortable, and confident. People often feel safe with parents and other family members, teachers, counselors, youth workers, leaders at a place of worship, and other trusted adults. Emphasize that it's the goal of staff to make sure that school is a place where students feel safe and able to do their best. Equate school with a safe harbor, a place where people don't have to worry about being harmed. Talk about how bullying hurts the school climate—it makes children fearful and doesn't allow for the focus to be on learning. (See "Bullying Basics" on pages 4–6 for more effects of and appropriate ways to respond to bullying.) As you work on this display, you can use questions like the following:

1. What is a harbor? Why do ships dock and anchor in a harbor?

2. What does it mean to say "our school is a safe, bully free harbor"?

3. What can each of us do to make our school a safer place where everyone feels accepted and respected? (For examples of positive actions, see "Bully Free Actions" on page 136.)

You can use this display to post rules and expectations you have for behavior in the classroom.

WHAT TO DO _ _ _ _ _ _ _ _ _ _ _ _ _ _ _

1. Cover the board with bulletin board paper.
2. Work with students to enlarge, copy, and cut out the letters for the display title from construction paper.
3. Help children enlarge, copy, and cut out the figures, desks, and rules sheet. Mount each of the pieces. (Desks should be placed over the figures, as shown.)
4. Mount the display title on the rules sheet and use a marker to write classroom rules.

Variation: This board can be modified for any school setting (including the lunchroom, gymnasium, or media center). Simply alter the bulletin board title and include rules appropriate for the desired location.

WHAT TO TALK ABOUT _ _ _ _ _ _ _ _ _

As you put together this display with students, talk about classroom rules and your expectations for behavior. (For examples, see "Rules for a Bully Free Classroom" on page 6.) Talk about why rules are important—they let us get along and help us feel safe and secure in the classroom. Involving students in the creation of rules can be a good way to encourage their following them. If they believe that they've had a part in setting expectations, they will be more likely to recognize them as important. Lead the discussion, offering a few rules you think are important. Then ask for their suggestions. Talk about why each rule is an important expectation for the classroom. You can use questions like the following:

1. Why is it important to follow rules in the classroom?
2. What happens when people don't follow rules?
3. What rules do you think our classroom needs? Why?

Ready...Set...Go!

Our Bus Is Bully Free

You can use this display to address bullying that occurs on the bus.

WHAT TO DO _____

1. Cover the board with bulletin board paper.

2. Work with children to enlarge, copy, and cut out the letters for the display title from construction paper and mount them on the board.

3. Help students to enlarge, copy, cut out, and mount the bus on the display.

Variation: Write out rules for riding the bus and post them on this display. Talk about why each rule is important for student safety on buses. (You may wish to adapt some of the rules from "Rules for a Bully Free Classroom" on page 6.) Post the display in an area where students wait to board the bus.

WHAT TO TALK ABOUT _____

As you assemble this display with students, talk about how bullying happens in places outside of the classroom—including on the bus. People sometimes kick or hit others, tease, or take others' things. Discuss why sitting quietly, respecting others (and their property), and keeping hands and feet to yourself are important. Talk about what can happen when behavior is a problem on the bus. People are hurt or upset and the driver cannot concentrate on driving—a bus with bullying isn't safe. As you discuss bullying on the bus, you can use questions like the following:

1. Bullying happens in places outside of school—including on the bus. What kind of bullying happens on the bus?

2. Why is sitting quietly (showing respect for others, keeping your hands to yourself) important on the bus?

3. What should you do if bullying happens on the bus? (See "Appropriate Student Responses to Bullying" on pages 4–5 for suggestions.)

Be a Good Friend

You can use this display to talk about the benefits of friendship and the qualities that make someone a good friend. You can also give students tools to overcome conflicts that occur between friends.

WHAT TO DO

1. Cover the board with bulletin board paper.

2. Work with students to enlarge, copy, and cut out the letters for the display title from construction paper and mount them on the board.

3. As needed, help children to enlarge, copy, and cut out the figures from construction paper. Ask students to use markers to customize their figures by adding clothing and other features.

4. Help students mount their figures on the board.

WHAT TO TALK ABOUT

As you put together this display with students, talk about friendship and its benefits. When we have friends, we feel happy, secure, confident, and cared for. Friends make life more fun and satisfying. Discuss the behaviors that a good friend shows. A friend is respectful, tells the truth, shares, and talks out problems instead of fighting. (See "Bully Free Actions" on page 136 for more positive actions friends do.) Also talk about problem behaviors that can hurt friendships—when, for example, friends share a personal secret, say something mean, or don't do what they say they will do. Discuss ways to get past conflicts (by talking about how you feel rather than blaming and listening closely to what another person is saying, for example). You can use questions like the following:

1. How do you feel when you are with friends? (For examples of emotions, see "Feelings" on page 138.)

2. What makes someone a good friend?

3. What kinds of things can hurt a friendship or keep people from making friends?

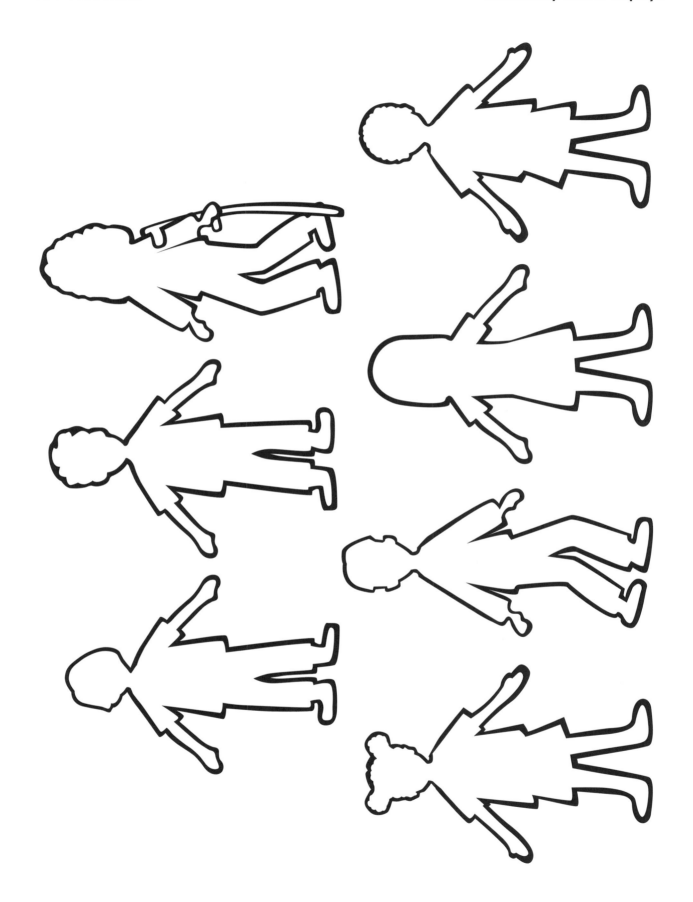

This display can be used to recognize the good deeds of students in your classroom.

WHAT TO DO _____

1. Cover the board with bulletin board paper.

2. Enlarge, copy, and cut out the letters for the display title from construction paper and mount them on the board.

3. Enlarge, copy, and cut out the scrolls from construction paper and mount them on the display as students are observed being kind. Use a marker to write students' names and kind actions on the scroll.

WHAT TO TALK ABOUT _____

As students are recognized for kind actions, discuss them in a group setting. Talk about why you are rewarding a student and how kind actions help not only individuals, but the entire class. When everyone is respectful and helpful, students feel secure and supported in class. Encourage others to perform good deeds, noting that others "caught being kind" will also be recognized. Help every student to feel involved by ensuring that all are acknowledged by the end of the week, month, or year (or however long you maintain the display). As you talk about students' kind actions, you can use questions like the following:

1. Why is Samantha (Robin, Juan) being recognized? How was Samantha's (Robin's, Juan's) action kind?

2. What are some other acts of kindness that you have seen? Has there been a time when you did something to help someone out?

3. How do kind actions make school a better place to learn?

Bully Free City

The buildings in the image are labeled: POSITIVE PLACE, GUIDANCE GARAGE, TOLERANCE TOWER, ASSURANCE AVENUE, PEACE PLAZA, DIGNITY DRIVE, RESPECT ROAD, KINDNESS COURT, SUPPORTIVE STREET

The purpose of this board is to show that—much like a town or city—a classroom needs to have rules and respectful behavior to run smoothly.

WHAT TO DO

1. Cover the board with bulletin board paper.

2. Enlarge, copy, and cut out the letters for the display title from construction paper and mount them on the board.

3. Invite students to create buildings out of construction paper. Ask them to use a marker to give their buildings names that incorporate positive, bully free qualities and actions ("Peace Plaza" or "Tolerance Tower," for example).

4. Help students mount the buildings on the board. Using markers, add streets with names that also incorporate positive qualities and actions ("Respect Road" or "Kindness Court," for example).

Variation: Rather than make the title of your display "Bully Free City," use the name of your state, province, or region (for example, "Bully Free, Ohio"). Likewise, you can use your state, provincial, or regional flag—or that of the country where you live.

WHAT TO TALK ABOUT

As you help students mount their buildings on the board, draw parallels between a city and a classroom. A city needs many offices, shops, and government buildings in order to be a good place to live and work. It also needs many rules. People driving have to follow the directions of street signs. It's important for customers in shops to wait in line for their turn. Classrooms depend on rules and respectful behavior, too. When we follow rules and treat each other well at school, we can feel safe, get along with each other, and focus on learning. As you assemble this display with students, you can use questions like the following:

1. What does it mean to be tolerant (kind, respectful)?

2. How do you feel when people are kind and respectful to you? How do you feel when people are disrespectful or mean?

3. What would happen if people in a city did not follow rules or show respectful behavior? What could happen in our classroom if we did not follow rules or show respect for each other?

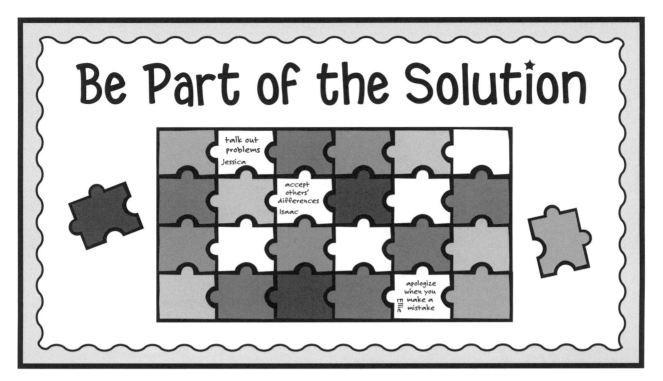

Be Part of the Solution

This display is intended to show students that they can play an important part in making classrooms safe, enjoyable places where the focus is on learning.

WHAT TO DO _ _ _ _ _ _ _ _ _ _ _ _ _ _ _ _

1. Cover the board with bulletin board paper.

2. Enlarge, copy, and cut out the letters for the display title from construction paper and mount them on the board.

4. Invite students to select a sheet of construction paper. Help children as needed to trace and cut out a puzzle piece. Ask them to use markers to add their names and bully free actions.

5. Help students to mount puzzle pieces on the board.

WHAT TO TALK ABOUT _ _ _ _ _ _ _ _ _

As you put together this display with students, talk about how everyone's positive behavior is important toward making the classroom a comfortable and secure place. Draw parallels between solving a puzzle and creating a safe, bully free classroom. Just like all of the pieces of a puzzle must be included for it to be solved, everyone's appropriate behavior is needed for a classroom to be caring and supportive. We are all "part of the solution." When students are ready to mount their puzzle pieces on the display, discuss the positive actions they have chosen to write. (For examples, see "Bully Free Actions" on page 136.) Talk about how each of the positive actions add up to the goal or solution—a bully free classroom. Use questions like the following:

1. What is one positive action you show to "be part of the solution"?

2. What happens when a puzzle piece is missing or out of place?

3. What happens when classroom behavior is inappropriate?

This display serves as a visible reminder that acting out violently is not acceptable and that there are peaceful ways to resolve conflicts.

WHAT TO DO _____

1. Cover the board with bulletin board paper.

2. Work with students to enlarge, copy, and cut out the letters for the display title from construction paper and mount them on the board.

3. Help students to enlarge, copy, and cut out the stoplight. (Use appropriately colored construction paper for lights—red for stop, yellow for think, green for decide.) Use markers to highlight the "Stop," "Think," and "Decide" lettering.

4. Mount the stoplight on the board.

WHAT TO TALK ABOUT _____

As you put together this display with students, talk about how it is easy for people to lose their cool, but that blowing up does not resolve conflicts—instead, it makes things worse. Discuss how using the "Stop, Think, Decide"

model can prevent a situation from getting out of control and lead to positive solutions to problems. Discuss common techniques for calming down—like deep breathing, counting backwards from ten, and visualizing yourself handling things calmly. Emphasize the importance of thinking about the consequences of actions and deciding to act in a way that can resolve a conflict—not escalate it. During this discussion, you can use questions like the following:

1. What happens when people lose their cool? How does blowing up make a situation worse?

2. Why is it a good idea to stop when you're getting upset, think about possible solutions, and decide to address a problem in a positive way?

3. Have you ever lost your cool or blown up at someone? What happened? What positive solution might you have tried instead?

You can use this board to broadly discuss bullying and send a clear visual message that it will not be tolerated at school.

WHAT TO DO _ _ _ _ _ _ _ _ _ _ _ _ _ _ _

1. Cover the board with bulletin board paper.

2. Help students to enlarge, copy, and cut out the letters for the display title from construction paper and mount them on the board.

3. Work with students to enlarge, copy, and cut out the "no" symbol.

4. Mount the "no" symbol on the board over the word "bullying."

WHAT TO TALK ABOUT _ _ _ _ _ _ _ _ _

As you put together this display with students, talk in depth about the kinds of bullying, its harmful effects, and what can be done to stop it. (For information, see "Bullying Basics" on pages 4–6.) Discuss the important role bystanders play in bullying, emphasizing that students should report all bullying incidents. Also encourage students to support those who have been bullied by being a friend to them. You can use questions like the following:

1. Why is it important that everyone feel safe, accepted, and respected at school?

2. Have you ever been bullied? What happened? How did you feel?

3. Have you ever seen someone else bullied? What did you do?

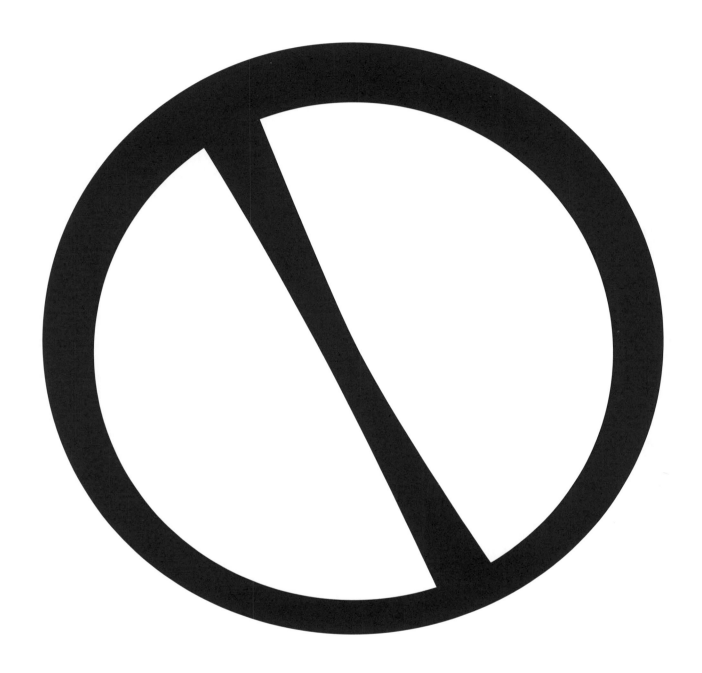

----------- MIDDLE SCHOOL -----------
DISPLAYS

Use this board to talk about bullying generally and your expectations for positive behavior in the school setting.

WHAT TO DO

1. Cover the board with bulletin board paper.

2. Work with students to enlarge, copy, and cut out the letters for the display title from construction paper and mount them on the board.

3. Work with your group to enlarge, copy, and cut out the figures from construction paper and mount them on the board. (Additional figures and accessories can be found throughout this book and on pages 134–135.)

Variation: This board can be modified for any school setting (including the lunchroom, gymnasium, media center, locker room, or hallways). Simply alter the display title to fit your needs.

WHAT TO TALK ABOUT

As you put together this display with students, talk about what bullying is, how it hurts people, and what should be done when it occurs. (See "Bullying Basics" on pages 4–6 for information.) Clearly communicate that bullying will not be tolerated in the classroom (lunchroom, gymnasium). Encourage those who are bullied—and those who observe bullying—to report all incidents. Finally, talk about your expectations for student behavior. Place your discussion of these expectations in the context of building community at school. When we all show respect for and support each other, the result is a safe and healthy learning environment where we are able to do our best. You can use questions like the following:

1. What is bullying? What are some bullying behaviors? How does bullying hurt people?

2. What should you do when you are bullied? What should you do when you see others bullied?

3. What are steps we can take as a group to create a bully free classroom (locker room, hallway)?

This display can be used to make it clear that bullying has very serious effects on individuals and the school environment.

WHAT TO DO _____

1. Cover the board with bulletin board paper.

2. Work with your group to enlarge, copy, and cut out the letters for the display title from construction paper and mount them on the board.

3. Work with students to enlarge, copy, and cut out the sports equipment from construction paper and mount it on the board.

Variation: Add your school's name, seal, or mascot to this display to customize it for your setting.

WHAT TO TALK ABOUT _____

As you put together this display with students, talk in depth about the kinds of bullying and the harmful effects bullying has on students and the school community. (For information, see "Bullying Basics" on pages 4–6.) Some who

bully others say things like, "I was just kidding around," "We were just having a little fun," or "She knows we don't mean it." Passing bullying off as some kind of game or form of recreation is wrong. Talk about how important it is for students to put themselves in the place of those who are bullied. Point out that people who suffer prolonged mistreatment are more likely to commit suicide, act out violently, use drugs and alcohol, and develop eating disorders and other health problems. Throughout your discussion, you can use questions like the following:

1. Why is bullying serious and not a game?

2. What kinds of problems occur in our school because of bullying?

3. Do you think that our school has problem with bullying? Why or why not? If you think bullying is a problem at school, what can we—students and teachers—do to address it?

Use this display to talk about the importance of showing others respect at school.

WHAT TO DO _ _ _ _ _ _ _ _ _ _ _ _ _ _ _ _

1. Cover the board with bulletin board paper.

2. Work with students to enlarge, copy, and cut out the letters for the display title from construction paper and mount them on the board.

3. Work with your group to enlarge, copy, and cut out the figures and podium from construction paper and mount them on the board.

WHAT TO TALK ABOUT _ _ _ _ _ _ _ _ _

As you put together this display with students, talk about why it's important to show others respect. When we respect others, they feel like they're important and belong at school. Giving others our respect shows that we value them as human beings. Discuss what happens when people show disrespectful behavior. People's feelings can be hurt, they don't feel supported, and conflicts can escalate. Emphasize that although we are different from each other in many ways, respect is something that we all need—and deserve. Throughout your discussion, you can use questions like the following:

1. What does respect mean to you?

2. Why is showing others respect important? How do you show respect?

3. Have you ever been disrespected? What happened? How did you feel?

Friends Don't Hurt Friends

You can use this display to address the disrespectful and cruel behavior that can result when popularity or wanting to fit into a certain clique drive friends apart.

WHAT TO DO

1. Cover the board with bulletin board paper.
2. Work with your group to enlarge, copy, and cut out the letters for the display title from construction paper and mount them on the board.
3. Work with students to enlarge, copy, and cut out the figures and signs from construction paper and mount them on the board.
4. Use markers to write anti-bullying messages on signs.

WHAT TO TALK ABOUT

As you put together this display with students, talk about how friends treat each other. Good friends support each other. They listen to and try to help each other out. Talk about how popularity and wanting to belong to a group can turn friends against each other and even lead to forms of bullying—including spreading rumors and excluding or intimidating others. Good friends don't turn against someone when they're with another person or group. Friends are always considerate and respectful, and they don't try to pressure people to do things they're not comfortable with. (For more examples of positive qualities that friends have, see "Bully Free Qualities" on page 137.) Talk about how disagreements occur between even best friends, but that they can be worked out by talking about how you feel and listening to the other person. During this discussion, you can use questions like the following:

1. What qualities do you look for in friends? What qualities make someone a good friend?
2. How can wanting to be popular or belong to a clique complicate friendships?
3. Have you ever mistreated someone to fit in with a group? What happened? How did you feel?

This display can be used to discuss bullying, including some of the reasons some students choose to bully.

WHAT TO DO _____

1. Cover the board with bulletin board paper.

2. Work with students to enlarge, copy, and cut out the letters for the display title from construction paper and mount them on the board.

3. Work with your group to enlarge, copy, and cut out the cheerleading figures from construction paper and mount them on the board.

Variation: Place your school's logo on cheerleaders' uniforms—or add the school mascot—to customize this display for your setting.

WHAT TO TALK ABOUT _____

As you put together this display with students, talk about what bullying is and what should be done when it occurs. (For background information, see "Bullying Basics" on pages 4–6.) Also discuss why some students bully others. Often students want to be liked by peers, but they don't know how to show it in positive ways. Encourage students—when it is safe to do so—to try to be friends with and include people who have previously shown bullying behaviors. Many children who mistreat others have themselves been bullied. They often feel hurt, frustrated, or helpless and believe the only way to feel better is by having power over others by bullying them. Communicate clearly that this is not acceptable—that there are positive ways to handle difficult feelings. (Distressed students can, for example, seek help from an adult.) You can use questions like the following:

1. What are some bullying behaviors? What should you do when bullying occurs?

2. Have you ever been mistreated? What happened? How did you feel?

3. Why do some students choose to bully others? What can we do to help those who show bullying behaviors?

Be an Ally to People Who Are Bullied

You can use this display to talk about the important role bystanders play in bullying and to empower students to speak out when they witness mistreatment.

WHAT TO DO _ _ _ _ _ _ _ _ _ _ _ _ _ _ _

1. Cover the board with bulletin board paper.

2. Work with your group to enlarge, copy, and cut out the letters for the display title from construction paper and mount them on the board.

3. Work with students to enlarge, copy, and cut out the figures from construction paper and mount them on the board.

WHAT TO TALK ABOUT _ _ _ _ _ _ _ _ _

As you put together this display with students, talk about how everyone has to work toward making a school bully free. It's not enough to simply refrain from harassing or hurting others—though that is a necessary first step.

Rather, everyone has a responsibility to report bullying and support those who've been bullied. Emphasize the major part bystanders play in bullying—and that silently allowing it to occur is a form of endorsement. Also talk about how students can support those who are bullied—by listening to them, including them in activities, and being a friend. During this discussion, you can use questions like the following:

1. Why is it important for bystanders to speak out against bullying and support those who have been bullied?

2. How can you be an ally—or friend—to someone who has been bullied?

3. How do reporting bullying and standing up for others who are bullied help make school a better place for everyone?

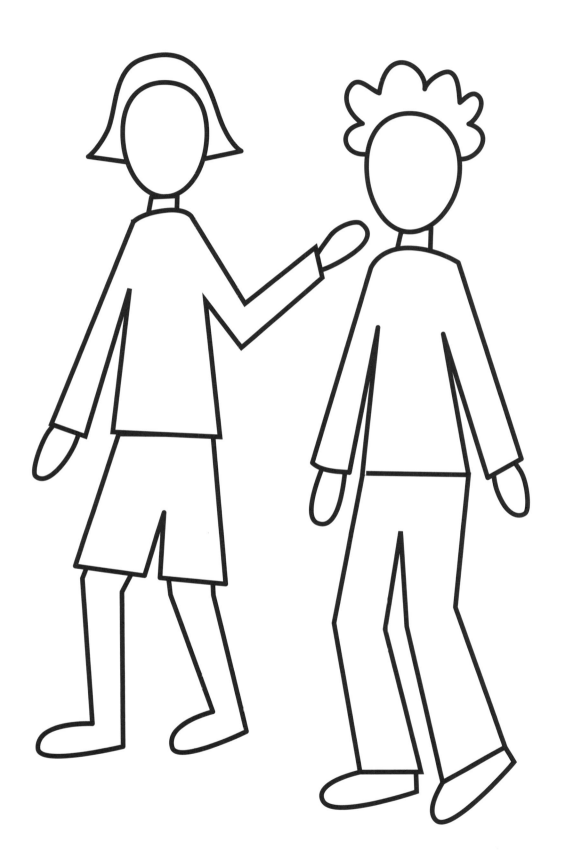

Free to Be Me...
Our School Is Bully Free

You can use this display to promote tolerance and help students celebrate their differences.

WHAT TO DO _____

1. Cover the board with bulletin board paper.

2. Work with students to enlarge, copy, and cut out the letters for the display title from construction paper and mount them on the board.

3. Work with your group to enlarge, copy, and cut out the figures from construction paper and mount them on the board.

4. Enlarge, copy, and cut out flag shapes. Ask students to use markers to decorate a flag for each nationality represented in the class.

Variation: If you've a fairly homogeneous classroom, students can create flags based on countries from which their ancestors came. Or flags can be created on the basis of other differences that you deem appropriate—students' different interests or talents, for example.

WHAT TO TALK ABOUT _____

As you assemble this display with students, talk about how we are different from one another. We may be from different ethnic, cultural, or religious backgrounds. We also may have different physical features, personalities, and interests. Emphasize that while we are different from each other in many ways, we are all human beings who deserve respect. It's important to remember that we all have thoughts and feelings—something that makes us more alike than different. When we accept and respect each other, we can appreciate and celebrate the things that make us different. Affirm that we should all feel proud of who we are. You can use questions like the following:

1. Why is it important to accept others? How does accepting others let us be ourselves?

2. Have you ever been targeted because you are different in some way? How did you feel? (For examples of emotions, see "Feelings" on page 138.)

3. Think of situations in history where a person or group of people was not respected or valued? What happened? What lessons can be learned from the situation?

We Band Together to Stop Bullying

You can use this display to emphasize the important part each student plays in creating a bully free classroom.

WHAT TO DO _ _ _ _ _ _ _ _ _ _ _ _ _

1. Cover the board with bulletin board paper.

2. Work with students to enlarge, copy, and cut out the letters for the display title from construction paper and mount them on the board.

3. Work with your group to enlarge, copy, and cut out the instruments. Mount them on the board.

4. Use markers to draw musical notes and positive, bully free qualities coming out of the instruments.

Variation: Customize this display by adding your school's name and logo or mascot.

WHAT TO TALK ABOUT_ _ _ _ _ _ _ _ _

As you put together this display with students, use the band metaphor to explain how each person doing his or her part to be kind and respectful makes for a group that gets along. Just as band members have to play correctly to perform well, students can work together to make life at school safe and enjoyable. Talk about the responsibility of the individual—emphasizing that we all control our own actions and that we should choose to make them friendly and helpful, not hurtful. Emphasize that not bullying others is not enough, but that reporting incidents and—if it is safe—stepping in to stop them are also necessary to help keep school bully free. When the board is completed, ask students what part they can play individually and as a group to make school a better place. Write some of these ideas on the board above instruments. Throughout your discussion, you can use questions like the following:

1. What happens when one member of a band is out of tune?

2. How must a band work together to create music?

3. What responsibility can you take to help your school be bully free?

Within the image:
Set up a pickup game of basketball
invite someone to lunch
connect with faraway friends
plan a party
create a Web site about a hobby

Bully Free Mail

Use this display to address cyber bullying—bullying that uses newer technologies like email and Web sites to hurt others.

WHAT TO DO

1. Cover the board with bulletin board paper.

2. Work with your group to enlarge, copy, and cut out the letters for the display title from construction paper and mount them on the board.

3. Work with students to enlarge, copy, and cut out the computer, keyboard, and mouse from construction paper and mount them on the board.

4. Use markers to write some positive things students can use email, Web sites, and instant messaging for on the computer screen.

WHAT TO TALK ABOUT

As you put together this display with students, talk about how some people use computers to intimidate, put down, or humiliate others. Cyber bullying can include spreading rumors by email, sending nasty messages or threats, and posting private or false information about people on Web sites. Emphasize that these forms of bullying are serious—they can be as or more damaging to people than bullying that takes place amongst peers. Encourage students not to join in cyber bullying, to speak out against it, and to report it. (You can recommend they save any emails and print off materials from Web sites so that they may show school staff.) During this discussion, you can use questions like the following:

1. What is cyber bullying? What are some of its forms?

2. Has anyone ever used cyber bullying to harass you? How did you feel?

3. How can students and staff work together

Get the 411...

Instead of:

spreading rumors

sending mean text messages

taking private photos

IM BULLY FREE

Make a better call:

call a friend or family member

send fun text messages

take pictures of good times with friends

No Bullying!

You can use this display to send a clear message that bullying others using cell phones is not acceptable.

WHAT TO DO _____

1. Cover the board with bulletin board paper.
2. Work with your group to enlarge, copy, and cut out the letters for the display title from construction paper and mount them on the board.
3. Work with students to enlarge, copy, and cut out the cell phone from construction paper and mount it on the board.
4. Use markers to write down some of the ways students use cell phones to bully others. Then write some positive ways cell phones can be used instead.

WHAT TO TALK ABOUT_____

As you put together this display with students, talk about the ways some people use cell phones to intimidate, put down, or humiliate others. People may use text messaging to send threats or spread rumors. Others may take inappropriate photos of people—such as in the locker room—to humiliate them. Repeatedly calling and hanging up on someone is another way cell phones are used to harass others. As you discuss cell-phone bullying, emphasize that it can be as hurtful as other forms of bullying and that it is not acceptable. Encourage students not to join in this form of bullying, to speak out against it, and to report it. (You can recommend they save any text messages and photos so that they may show school staff.) You can use questions like the following:

1. How do some people use cell phones to intimidate, put down, or tease others?
2. Has anyone ever used cell-phone bullying to harass you? How did you feel? (For examples of emotions, see "Feelings" on page 138.)
3. What can you do to stop cell-phone bullying?

Our Goal? Stop Bullying Now!

This display can send an effective anti-bullying message in places at school where sports-related activities are taking place—like gymnasiums and locker rooms.

WHAT TO DO

1. Cover the board with bulletin board paper.

2. Work with students to enlarge, copy, and cut out the letters for the display title from construction paper and mount them on the board.

3. Work with your group to enlarge, copy, and cut out the soccer net, goalie, and ball patterns. Use markers to decorate the goalie in your school's colors or uniform.

4. Mount the soccer net, goalie, and ball on the board.

WHAT TO TALK ABOUT

As you put together this display with students, talk about proper behavior in physical education and sports settings. Often poor sportsmanship—putting others down, cheating, bragging, and physical fighting—makes its way into games or play. Talk about how following the rules, treating others with respect, and being a gracious winner make games more fun for everyone. Also discuss how locker rooms are often places where people are harassed or physically hurt. You can bring up high-profile instances of hazing—team "initiation rites" intended to humiliate—that have brought nationwide attention to the problem. Emphasize the importance of showing respectful behavior on the field, in the gymnasium, and in the locker room. Throughout this discussion, you can use questions like the following:

1. What conflicts can come up in physical education classes and sports events? Why is it important to show good sportsmanship?

2. What is hazing? Why is hazing wrong?

3. What can school staff and coaches do to address bullying that happens during physical education classes and sporting events?

UNITY Won't Work Without "U"

Use this display to emphasize the important role every student plays in making school a safe and enjoyable place to be.

WHAT TO DO

1. Cover the board with bulletin board paper.

2. Work with your group to enlarge, copy, and cut out the letters for the display title from construction paper and mount them on the board.

3. Work with students to enlarge, copy, and cut out the figures and mount them on the board.

4. Use markers to add "UNITY" lettering to figures.

WHAT TO TALK ABOUT

As you put together this display with students, talk about unity and how people can work individually to meet the goals of a group. You can use the analogy of a sports team—individual team members have specific responsibilities they perform to try and help the team win.

Similarly, students can make individual efforts within the classroom or school toward creating a positive learning environment. Students can be kind, considerate, and empathetic. (For more qualities that promote unity, see "Bully Free Qualities" on page 137.) They can speak out when others are mistreated, report bullying incidents, and make an effort to include those who are often teased or left out. Talk about how all of these individual actions help toward the goal of your school: that it be a place where all are accepted and valued. You can use questions like the following:

1. Why is it important that we all work to stop bullying at our school?

2. Why does bullying or harm against one individual hurt the entire class and school?

3. What can you do to be a leader in working toward a bully free school?

Use this board to talk about the importance of tolerance and discuss how it empowers us to be our best.

WHAT TO DO ─ ─ ─ ─ ─ ─ ─ ─ ─ ─

1. Cover the board with bulletin board paper.

2. Work with students to enlarge, copy, and cut out the letters for the display title from construction paper and mount them on the board.

3. Work with your group to enlarge, copy, and cut out the figures from construction paper. Students can decorate figures with symbols to represent different ethnic, religious, and cultural groups.

4. Mount the figures on the board.

WHAT TO TALK ABOUT ─ ─ ─ ─ ─ ─ ─

As you assemble this display with students, talk about tolerance. Because we're different from each other in many ways—we have different physical features, interests, and cultural, religious, and ethnic backgrounds—accepting others is important toward letting us live well together. If tolerance were not a priority for society, any individual could be put down or persecuted for having particular physical traits or beliefs. When we accept and respect everyone, we are respecting ourselves. You may wish to talk about how differences between people have throughout history been used to justify demonizing or persecuting others. Affirm that we can be proud of who we are, but also open-minded about others and the way they live. During this discussion, you can use questions like the following:

1. What is tolerance? How is tolerance powerful?

2. Have you ever experienced or witnessed intolerance? How did you feel? (For examples of emotions, see "Feelings" on page 138.)

3. Think of situations in history where a person or group of people was persecuted because of intolerance. What happened? What lessons can be learned?

Take a Stand...
Give Someone
a Hand!

Use this display to discuss the important role bystanders can have in stopping bullying and making everyone feel welcome at school.

WHAT TO DO _ _ _ _ _ _ _ _ _ _ _ _ _ _ _

1. Cover the board with bulletin board paper.

2. Work with your group to enlarge, copy, and cut out the letters for the display title from construction paper and mount them on the board.

3. Work with students to enlarge, copy, and cut out the figures and backpack materials. Mount them on the board.

WHAT TO TALK ABOUT _ _ _ _ _ _ _ _ _

As you put together this display with students, talk about the importance of speaking out against bullying and standing up for those who are bullied. Emphasize that students should step in if it's safe for them to do so. If it is not, they should get help from an adult immediately. (For more information on bullying and appropriate

responses to it, see "Bullying Basics" on pages 4–6.) Discuss how individual efforts to be kind to and include those who are bullied can go far toward reducing the pain they experience. Talk about how small acts, like sitting with a person at lunch or inviting them to join in an after-school game, can make students who are bullied feel welcome and increase their sense of belonging at school. You can use questions like the following:

1. Why are bystanders—those who witness bullying—important toward ending bullying at school?

2. Have you ever stood up for someone who was being bullied? How did you feel?

3. Why do some people not report bullying? What can happen when people aren't willing to speak out against or report bullying?

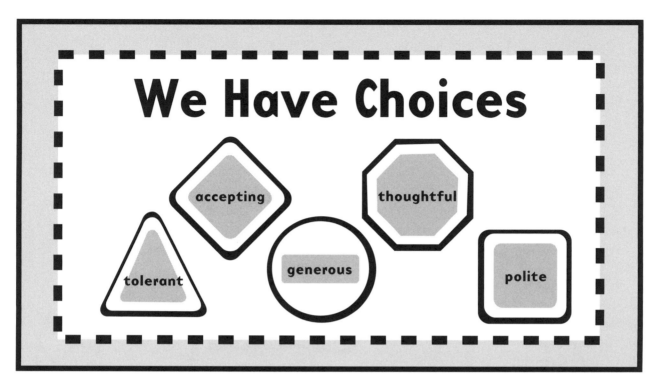

You can use this display to help students recognize that they have power over their behavior and that their individual actions have an impact on the school environment.

WHAT TO DO _ _ _ _ _ _ _ _ _ _ _ _ _ _

1. Cover the board with bulletin board paper.

2. Work with students to enlarge, copy, and cut out the letters for the display title from construction paper and mount them on the board.

3. Work with your group to enlarge, copy, and cut out the signs from construction paper.

4. Ask students for positive qualities and values that they stand for and choose to show. Ask them to add these qualities to the signs they have cut out.

5. Mount the signs on the board.

WHAT TO TALK ABOUT _ _ _ _ _ _ _ _ _

As you put together this display with students, talk about each of the qualities they chose to add to the signs. Examples of positive qualities are tolerant, accepting, polite, generous, and thoughtful. (For more examples, see "Bully Free Qualities" on page 137.) Emphasize that we all have control over how we treat others—that we can show we accept and value them. Talk about how choosing to show positive qualities makes school a safer and more pleasant place where everyone can be their best. During this discussion, you can use questions like the following:

1. What does it mean to be polite (tolerant, accepting, thoughtful)? Why is it important?

2. Has there been a time when you were generous (tolerant, accepting, thoughtful)? How did you feel? (For examples of emotions, see "Feelings" on page 138.)

3. How does showing positive qualities improve school for everyone?

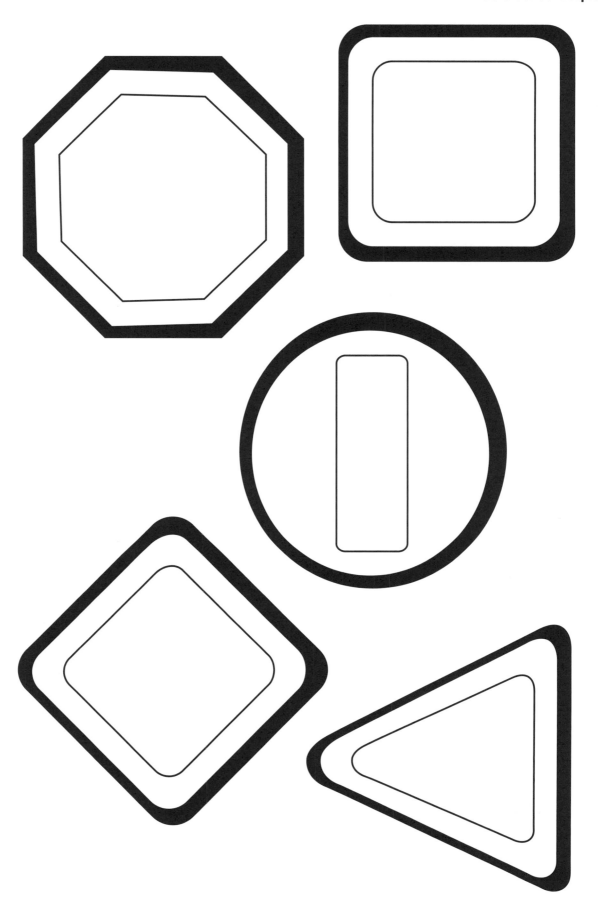

Use this display to broadly discuss bullying with students and to send a clear visual message that it will not be tolerated.

WHAT TO DO __ __ __ __ __ __ __ __

1. Cover the board with bulletin board paper.

2. Work with your group to enlarge, copy, and cut out the stop sign from construction paper and mount it on the board.

3. Work with students to enlarge, copy, and cut out the letters for the display from construction paper and mount them on the board.

WHAT TO TALK ABOUT __ __ __ __ __

As you put together this display with students, talk about what bullying is, its harmful effects, and appropriate responses to it. (See "Bullying Basics" on pages 4–6 for information.) Clearly communicate that bullying behaviors are not acceptable. Emphasize the importance of reporting all bullying incidents and showing kindness to those who are mistreated. Talk about what can happen when bullying is not reported—people who are bullied often suffer in silence and become isolated, lonely, overly anxious, or depressed. Some people who are bullied over long periods of time even commit suicide or act out violently at school. Those who are bullied, though, aren't the only people affected. No one at school is able to feel safe when there is a climate of fear. During your discussion of bullying, you can use questions like the following:

1. What are some bullying behaviors? What should people do when bullying occurs? What should people not do?

2. What can happen to people who are bullied over long periods of time?

3. Do you think there is a bullying problem at our school? Why or why not? What can we—students and staff—do together to stop all bullying?

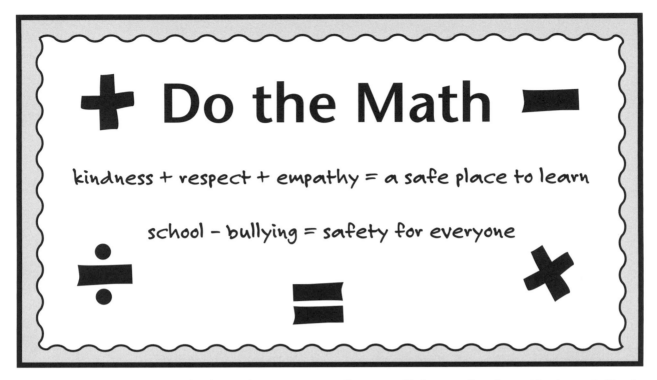

+ Do the Math ▬

kindness + respect + empathy = a safe place to learn

school − bullying = safety for everyone

You can use this bulletin board to promote key qualities and values that contribute to a safe learning environment.

WHAT TO DO _ _ _ _ _ _ _ _ _ _ _ _ _

1. Cover the board with bulletin board paper.
2. Work with students to enlarge, copy, and cut out the letters for the display title from construction paper and mount them on the board.
3. Work with your group to enlarge and cut out the math symbols from construction paper and mount them on the board.
4. Ask students to use markers to write positive qualities that "add up" to a bully free environment.

Variation: Have students create their own posters using math formulas. You might organize a contest and post students' work around different parts of the school.

WHAT TO TALK ABOUT _ _ _ _ _ _ _ _ _

As you put together this display with students, discuss the positive qualities they've chosen to include on the board. (For examples, see "Bully Free Qualities" on page 137.) Talk about how these qualities can "add up" to a safe learning environment. If you are able, bring up recent student actions that have exemplified the qualities. Talk about the consequences that come with not observing key classroom values. For example, not treating people with respect not only hurts others' feelings, but can also lead to arguments and physical conflicts. Throughout your discussion, you can use questions like the following:

1. What is kindness (empathy, respect)? Why is it important to show at school?
2. How does showing kindness (empathy, respect) make school a safer, more peaceful place?
3. What can happen when people do not show positive, bully free qualities at school?

BE A GOOD SPORT!

You can create this display with students in gymnasiums or recreation areas to promote good sportsmanship.

WHAT TO DO _____

1. Cover the board with bulletin board paper.
2. Work with your group to enlarge, copy, and cut out the letters for the display title from construction paper and mount them on the board.
3. Work with students to enlarge, copy, and cut out the figures from construction paper and mount them on the board.

WHAT TO TALK ABOUT _____

As you put together this display with students, talk about sportsmanship and how it makes games more enjoyable for everyone playing. Good sportsmanship means following all of the rules of a game, letting others play a part on a team, avoiding arguments, encouraging teammates, treating everyone (including those on an opposing team) with respect, and following the judgment of referees, coaches, and teachers. Good sports are also gracious winners and losers; they don't brag if they win a game or complain that the other team cheated if they lose. When people are not good sports, bullying behaviors can result. Emphasize that the point of playing sports and games should be to have fun, and that the quest to win doesn't justify causing fights or treating others badly. During this discussion on sportsmanship, you can use questions like the following:

1. What does it mean to be a good sport?
2. What can happen when people are bad sports?
3. Have you ever been part of a game where people began fighting or disrespecting each other? What happened? How could the situation have been avoided?

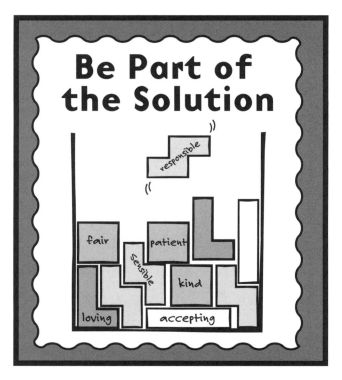

Be Part of the Solution

responsible

fair

patient

sensible

kind

loving

accepting

Use this display to demonstrate that everyone plays an important part in making the classroom a bully free environment.

WHAT TO DO

1. Cover the board with bulletin board paper.

2. Work with students to enlarge, copy, and cut out the letters for the display title from construction paper and mount them on the board.

3. Work with your group to enlarge, copy, and cut out the game shapes from construction paper.

4. Ask students to write positive, bully free qualities on game pieces and mount them on the board.

WHAT TO TALK ABOUT

As you put together this display with students, talk about how everyone must show positive qualities in the classroom if it's to be a safe and supportive environment. Responsible, cooperative, and understanding are all qualities that can help. (For more examples, see "Bully Free Qualities" on page 137.) Use the analogy of solving a video game puzzle—just like all of the pieces in a video game puzzle must be put together correctly for someone to get a high score, everyone's positive behavior in the classroom is needed for students to feel accepted and able to achieve their best. If only one piece of the video game puzzle is out of place, the game can be over. If only one person's behavior isn't appropriate, others can be hurt—and learning suffers because focus is on behavior, not the curriculum. In this way, we are all "part of the solution." Discuss each of the positive qualities students write on game shapes, and talk about how each promotes a better classroom environment. You can use questions like the following:

1. What are some positive qualities that we can show to "be part of the solution"?

2. What happens when classroom rules and expectations are not followed?

3. How can we all work together to make sure our classroom and school are places where everyone gets along and the focus is on learning?

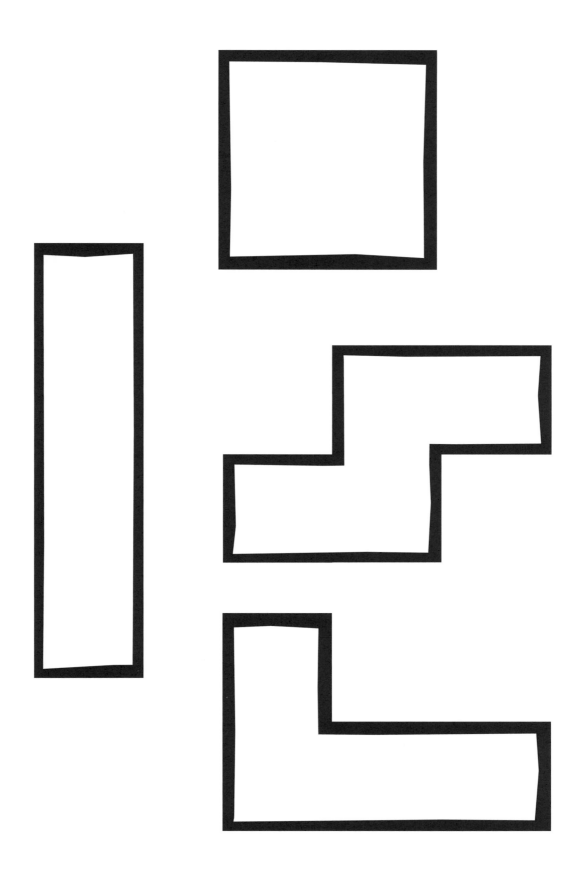

You can use this board to emphasize the important role bystanders can play in stopping bullying.

WHAT TO DO ----------------

1. Cover the board with bulletin board paper.

2. Work with your group to enlarge, copy, and cut out the letters for the display title from construction paper and mount them on the board.

3. Work with students to enlarge, copy, and cut out the figure and talk balloon from construction paper and mount them on the board.

4. Write an anti-bullying message in the talk balloon.

WHAT TO TALK ABOUT----------

As you put together this display with students, talk about why it's important that everyone be involved in creating a safe school. Often teachers do not see bullying, but students do. When bullying is observed, bystanders have a responsibility to try to stop it, if it is safe for them to do so. In situations where bystanders don't feel safe intervening, they should get the help of a teacher immediately. (For additional information on bullying and appropriate responses to it, see "Bullying Basics" on pages 4–6.) Talk about how students who are not bullied can help those who are in other ways. Students can invite others who are often left out to join in activities and spend time with them. Emphasize that being a friend to someone is a strong antidote to the damage bullying can cause. During this discussion, you can use questions like the following:

1. Why is it important for bystanders to speak out against bullying?

2. What are some ways you can support people who have been bullied?

3. How do the efforts of bystanders who report bullying help to improve the school climate?

Bully Free Message of the Week:

Treat others as you would like to be treated.

You can create this reusable display in any school area and routinely change the message to reflect your school's anti-bullying focus for a particular week.

WHAT TO DO _____

1. Cover the board with bulletin board paper.
2. Work with students to enlarge, copy, and cut out the letters for the display title from construction paper and mount them on the board.
3. Work with your group to enlarge, copy, and cut out the figures from construction paper and mount them on the board.
4. Select a bully free message and write it on construction paper. Mount the construction paper on the board. Bully free messages may be points of focus from an anti-bullying program you are currently using at your school, or simply key concepts that you feel are important. You can also consider using titles from displays that appear in this book.
5. Update the board weekly with a new message of acceptance.

Variation: Alter the title of this display to meet your needs. For example, if you'd like to change the message monthly—rather than weekly—create letters for the title "Bully Free Message of the Month."

WHAT TO TALK ABOUT _____

As you put together this display with students, talk about the harmful effects of and appropriate responses to bullying. Speaking out against bullying, reporting it to teachers, and being kind to those who have been bullied are all important. (See "Bullying Basics" on pages 4–6 for more information.) After talking about bullying and appropriate responses to it, discuss with students the bully free message that you've chosen to highlight for the week. You can use questions like the following:

1. Why is it important to be kind (treat others with respect, include people who are often left out)?
2. What can we do to be kind (treat others with respect, include people who are often left out)?
3. Have you ever seen others bullied? What did you do? What would you do today?

It's Not Cool to Be Cruel

You can use this display to talk about how some groups—or cliques—harm, tease, and exclude others.

WHAT TO DO

1. Cover the board with bulletin board paper.
2. Work with students to enlarge, copy, and cut out the figures and talk balloon from construction paper and mount them on the board.
3. Work with your group to enlarge, copy, and cut out the letters for the display title from construction paper and mount them on the board.

WHAT TO TALK ABOUT

As you put together this display with students, talk about how some groups—or cliques—hurt, exclude, threaten, taunt, or spread rumors about others. Cliques aren't necessarily bad—many are simply groups of people who share common interests. When people act like they are "better than" others or put them down because they aren't in a particular group, however, it's bullying. Emphasize that these kinds of behaviors can have very serious effects on the people who experience them. Many of the students involved in high-profile incidents of school violence, for example, were mistreated by peers over long periods of time. Having different interests and close friends is okay—disrespecting and putting others down isn't. Talk about how including others who are often teased or left out can make a big difference in how they feel at school. During your discussion, you can use questions like the following:

1. Why do people in some groups—or cliques—hurt, exclude, and put down others?
2. Have you ever been hurt or harassed by people who were in a clique? How did you feel? (For examples of emotions, see "Feelings" on page 138.)
3. How do harassment, exclusion, and taunting affect the learning environment? How can we work together to stop these behaviors from happening?

Lead the Way to Being Bully Free

You can use this display to talk about how important individual efforts are toward creating a safe and bully free school environment.

WHAT TO DO _ _ _ _ _ _ _ _ _ _ _ _ _ _ _ _ _

1. Cover the board with bulletin board paper.

2. Work with your group to enlarge, copy, and cut out the figures and arrow from construction paper and mount them on the board.

3. Work with students to enlarge, copy, and cut out the letters for the display title from construction paper and mount them on the board.

WHAT TO TALK ABOUT_ _ _ _ _ _ _ _ _

As you put together this display with students, talk about personal power and how we all can have a positive effect on the school climate. When individuals report bullying, speak out against it, and make an effort to include others, the whole school community benefits. People who bully often will continue to mistreat others when no one speaks out against their behavior. They may think that silence is tacit approval of their actions. One person speaking up, though, can have a large impact. Many other students— those who disapprove of bullying behaviors but are afraid to be the first to say anything—will likely join in. Throughout your discussion, you can use questions like the following:

1. Why is it important to stand up and speak out against bullying?

2. How does standing up for others who are bullied help everyone at school?

3. What can you do to help lead efforts toward a bully free school?

This display can be used to broadly discuss bullying, its harmful effects, and actions that should be taken when it occurs.

WHAT TO DO ----------------

1. Cover the board with bulletin board paper.

2. Work with your group to enlarge, copy, and cut out the letters for the display title from construction paper and mount them on the board.

3. Work with students to enlarge, copy, and cut out the dancing figures, disco ball, and stars from construction paper and mount them on the board.

WHAT TO TALK ABOUT---------

As you put together this display with students, talk about how bullying negatively affects the school climate. When a school has a bullying problem, students are fearful that they may be targeted. (Many miss school because they are afraid they will be bullied.) Rather than focus on schoolwork and school activities, students must instead worry about their safety. Alternatively, talk about how students feel when school is a safe and supportive place. When they're confident they will be accepted by others, students know that they can be themselves, have fun with others, and concentrate on their studies and extracurricular activities. Talk about ways that students can work together to make everyone feel welcome. During this discussion, you can use questions like the following:

1. What happens when students don't feel safe at school?

2. How does a bully free environment let everybody do and be their best?

3. What can you do to help make school a more enjoyable place for everyone? What can school staff do?

You Have Power Over Your Actions

You can use this display to talk with students about the importance of dealing with anger, frustration, and other difficult feelings in positive ways.

WHAT TO DO ─ ─ ─ ─ ─ ─ ─ ─ ─ ─ ─ ─

1. Cover the board with bulletin board paper.

2. Work with students to enlarge, copy, and cut out the letters for the display title from construction paper and mount them on the board.

3. Work with your group to enlarge, copy, and cut out the figure and stars and mount them on the board.

WHAT TO TALK ABOUT ─ ─ ─ ─ ─ ─ ─ ─ ─

As you put together this display with students, affirm that they have control over their actions. Emphasize that striking out physically—even when provoked—can only escalate conflicts. Let them know that it's okay to feel frustrated and angry—these are emotions that we all sometimes feel—but that there are positive ways to deal with strong feelings. Give students ideas for calming down when they're upset. (Deep breathing, counting backwards, and visualizing yourself handling things calmly are a few common ways.) Emphasize that acting out physically when provoked by someone signifies giving power to them. Suggest that students instead calm down and think about positive, nonviolent ways they can solve a conflict (talking in a calm voice about what they are feeling or telling a teacher what has happened, for example). You can use questions like the following:

1. What happens when people get frustrated or angry?

2. What are some positive ways you can deal with conflict?

3. How can you maintain power over your behavior—even when you're upset?

The bulletin board ideas from the previous section can easily be adapted into posters. Rather than placing lettering and art to a fixed board at your school, simply use tag board, construction paper, or another format that meets your needs as a base. Appropriately downsize lettering and art templates, glue or tape everything together, and you're done.

Posters are useful in that they are very mobile and can be created individually. Following are samples of poster-sized displays based on bulletin boards from the previous section. You can also feel free and encourage students to create unique posters. Mix and match ideas and elements from the preceding bulletin boards. Have a contest, if you like. Try to get everyone involved in talking about bullying and creating displays toward stopping it.

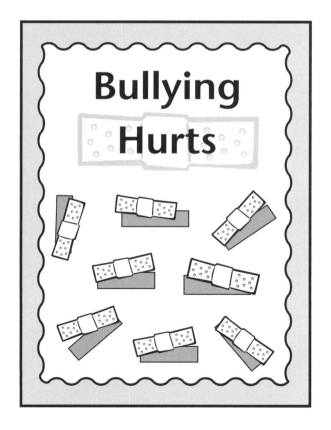

Like Snowflakes, We're Unique!

We Believe in Peace

OUR SCHOOL IS A SAFE, BULLY FREE HARBOR

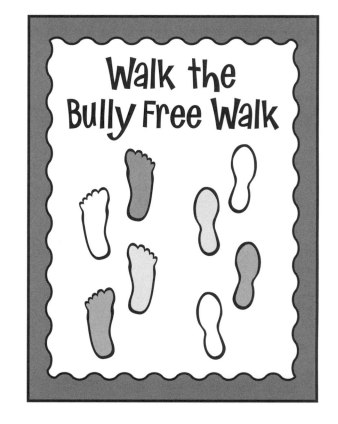

Walk the Bully Free Walk

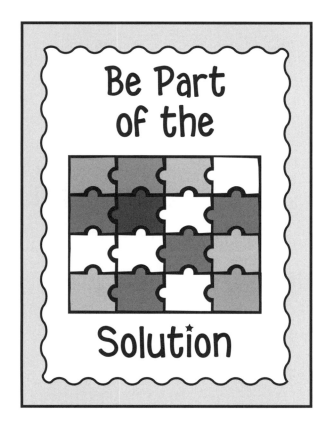

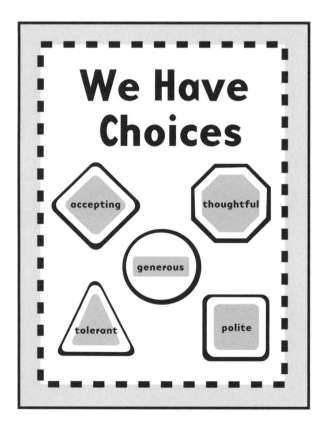

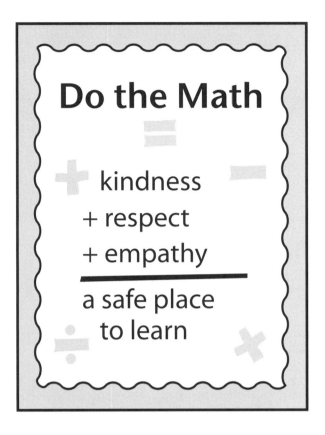

Banners can be created using the banner template on page 127 and the alphabets on pages 130–133. Use the overhead projector to enlarge and copy slogans in the same way you would in creating bulletin boards. You can use titles of bulletin boards from pages 8–108, slogans that you or students come up with, or pick from those that follow. It's all up to you!

There Is Great Strength in Being Kind

Our Path to Power?
We Don't Bully Others

WE TALK OUT OUR PROBLEMS

We Believe in Accepting Others

Treating Others with Respect...
It's About Being Grown Up

It's Not Cool to Be Cruel

Respect Yourself by Respecting Others

We Treat Each Other with Respect

We Like You Just the Way You Are!

WE DON'T MISTREAT OTHERS

Hurray for Differences!

Together We Can Make It Happen...
Be Bully Free

We Don't **All** Have to **Think** the **Same**

Bring Your "**A Game**" to School...
Speak Out Against Bullying

WE SPEAK UP IF WE SEE OTHERS TREATED UNFAIRLY

Bullying Hurts Everyone at School...
Speak Up Now!

WE DON'T ALL HAVE TO BE THE SAME

We Don't All Have to Talk the Same

We Have the Right to Be Ourselves

We Treat Each Other
the Way We'd Like to Be Treated

WE SOLVE PROBLEMS PEACEFULLY

Our Differences Make Us
Interesting and Unique

We Don't All Have to Believe the Same Things

We Don't All Have to Act the Same

Help Us to Be Bully Free

We Don't All Have to Dress the Same

We've Got the Right Stuff...We Don't Bully

Don't Just Stand By...
REPORT ALL BULLYING

WE'RE MORE ALIKE THAN DIFFERENT

Respect Yourself by Respecting Others

How We Treat Others Tells Us Who We Are

Do the Right Thing...
Report All Bullying

STOP Bullying Must Stop Now! STOP

NO ONE DESERVES TO BE BULLIED

We Can Work Out Our Problems

Fighting Back Is Still Fighting

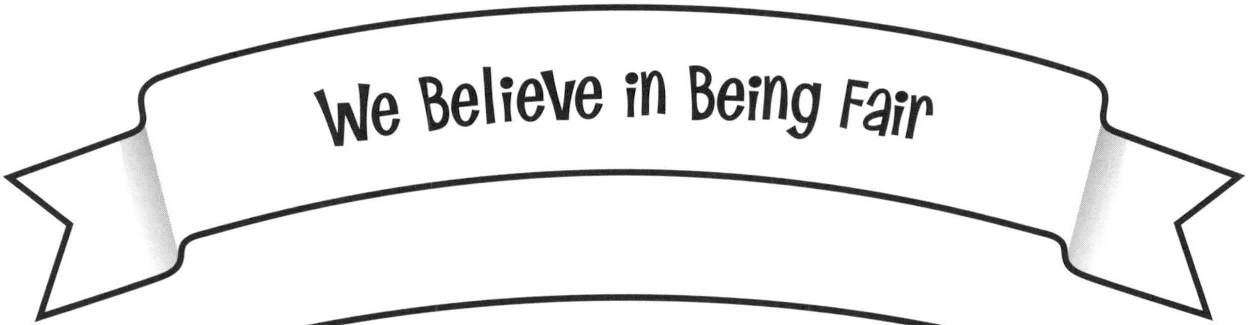

We Believe in Being Fair

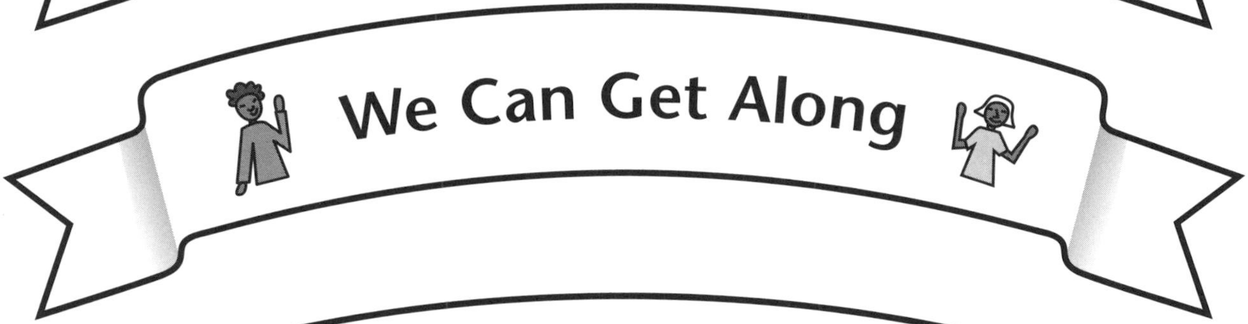

We Can Get Along

Assert Yourself!
Say No to Bullying

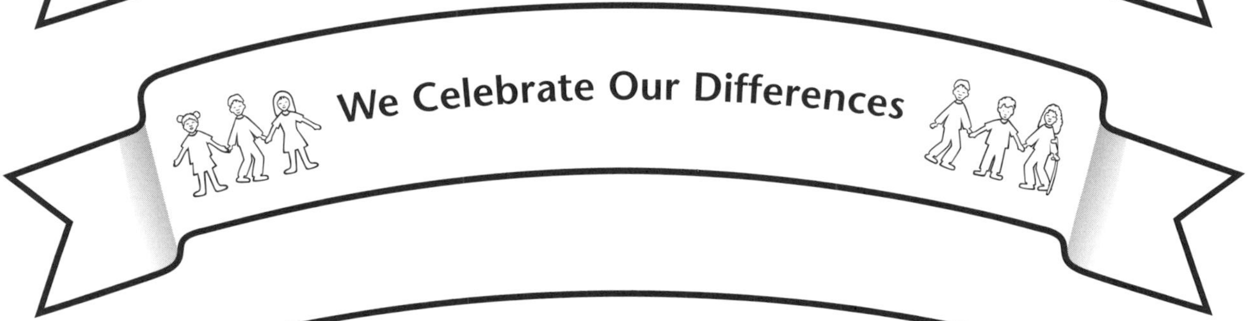

We Celebrate Our Differences

We're Better Than Bullying

We All Pitch in to Stop Bullying

We Keep Our Hands and Feet to Ourselves

WELCOME TO OUR BULLY FREE SCHOOL

We've Got Bully Free Spirit!

We Have Respect for Everyone

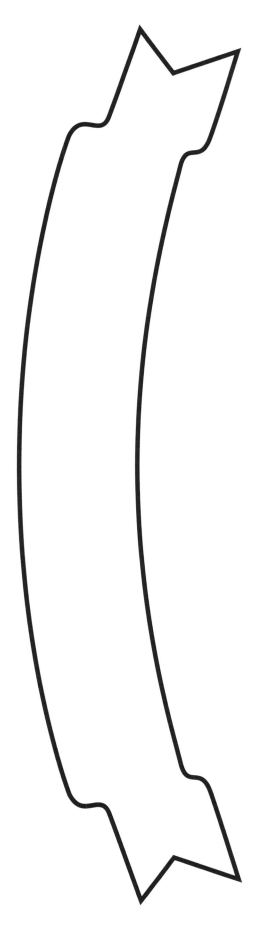

TOOLS

A B C D E F G H I J

K L M N O P Q R S

T U V W X Y Z

a b c d e f g h i j k

l m n o p q r s t u

v w x y z

1 2 3 4 5 6 7 8 9 0

? ! . , : & ' " "

A B C D E F G H I
J K L M N O P Q R
S T U V W X Y Z

a b c d e f g h i
j k l m n o p q r
s t u v w x y z

1 2 3 4 5 6 7 8
9 0 ? ! . , : & '
" "

A B C D E F G H I J
K L M N O P Q R S
T U V W X Y Z

a b c d e f g h i j
k l m n o p q r s t
u v w x y z

1 2 3 4 5 6 7 8 9
0 ? ! . , : & ' " "

A B C D E F G H I J
K L M N O P Q R S
T U V W X Y Z

a b c d e f g h i j
k l m n o p q r s t
u v w x y z

1 2 3 4 5 6 7 8 9
0 ? ! . , : & ' " "

--------- BULLY FREE ACTIONS ---------

say please, thank you, and other polite words

listen quietly when others are speaking

smile at people

try to understand how others feel

ask others to join in games and activities

take turns

share

tell the truth

help others

talk out problems (instead of fighting)

look others in the eye when you speak to them

show others respect

cooperate with others

encourage others

be friendly

do what you say you will do

use kind greetings like hi, hello, and good morning

apologize when you make a mistake

compromise

treat others fairly

solve problems peacefully

speak in a calm voice

listen to teachers

ask permission to use others' things

pay attention

treat objects at school with respect

talk about how you feel instead of blaming others

play fairly

follow the rules

keep your hands and feet to yourself

sit still in class

be careful with others' belongings

make others feel important

listen to others when they seem upset

give compliments

stand up for others who are picked on

report all bullying incidents

accept others' differences

do kind things for others

take deep breaths if you are angry

invite people to join you at lunch

speak positively about others

play nicely with others

keep your place in line (rather than budge)

help people who are having a conflict

be patient with others

congratulate others on achievements

show others that you care about them

-------- BULLY FREE QUALITIES --------

appreciative	gentle	reasonable
assertive	giving	reliable
aware	good sport	resilient
calm	helpful	responsible
caring	honest	sensible
cheerful	kind	sensitive
confident	loving	sharing
considerate	loyal	sincere
cooperative	mature	stable
courageous	mediator	thankful
courteous	nice	thoughtful
empathetic	open-minded	tolerant
fair	patient	trusting
faithful	peaceful	trustworthy
friendly	polite	understanding
generous	problem solver	unselfish

FEELINGS

afraid	furious	quiet
angry	glad	relaxed
annoyed	guilty	sad
anxious	happy	safe
calm	helpless	secure
confident	inspired	shaky
confused	lonely	shocked
content	lost	shy
cranky	lucky	surprised
dazzled	mad	tense
depressed	mellow	terrified
distracted	mixed-up	thankful
down	optimistic	tired
eager	panicked	trusting
embarrassed	pleased	upset
excited	proud	worried

Allan L. Beane, Ph.D., is a nationally recognized expert on the topic of bullying. He has over 30 years of experience in education that includes teaching special education, teaching regular education, and serving as director of a school safety center. Author of *The Bully Free Classroom*™ and other books, Allan has spoken and trained staff on bullying in many schools, and has served as an expert witness in criminal cases involving student mistreatment.

Linda Beane has over 20 years of experience in educational settings. Also a mother and grandmother, Linda has been widely recognized for her support of children and her responsiveness to their needs.

Allan and Linda operate Bully Free Systems, a company dedicated to preventing bullying in schools. Since the death of their son Curtis, in whose death bullying played a part, they have devoted their lives to creating safe and supportive learning environments where all students can be and achieve their best. For information on speaking, training, and workshop opportunities, visit www.bullyfree.com.

Other Bully Free® Products from Free Spirit

The Bully Free Classroom® (Book with CD-ROM)
by Allan L. Beane, Ph.D.
Bullying is a big problem in schools today. Allan Beane spells out more than 100 prevention and intervention strategies you can start using immediately. This solutions-filled book can make your classroom a place where all students are free to learn without fear—and you're free to teach because education, not behavior, is the focus. Includes 45 pages of reproducible handout masters. For grades K–8.
176 pp., softcover, illust., 8½" x 11." Macintosh and Windows compatible CD-ROM

Bully Free Zone® Poster and Bully Free Classroom® Poster
These big, bright posters send a positive message: This is a place where everyone belongs and no one is bullied (or bullies others). *17" x 22"*

Bully Free® Mini-Guides
by Allan L. Beane, Ph.D.
Support schools' anti-bullying efforts with four brochures from the author of *The Bully Free Classroom®*. Each features basic information about bullying and prevention written for a specific audience: students in grades K–3; students in grades 4–8; parents; and educators.
Sold in packets of 25

Bully Free® Card Game
Bullying is not a game—but helping kids learn anti-bullying concepts can be. Meant to be played with adult supervision (a teacher, counselor, or youth worker familiar with anti-bullying themes), the game includes an insert with rules and basic anti-bullying concepts. For grades K–8.
Pack of 60 cards and 12-page fold-out insert, color, 3" x 4½"

Good-Bye Bully Machine
by Debbie Fox and Allan L. Beane, Ph.D., illustrated by Debbie Fox
Kids learn what bullying is, why it hurts, and what they can do to end it with this fresh, compelling book. With its sophisticated collage art, lively layout, and straightforward text, *Good-Bye Bully Machine* engages kids and keeps them engaged. Adults who share this book with kids can raise awareness and increase empathy by talking about bullying behaviors as fuel for the machine—and kind behaviors as ways to dismantle it. For ages 8 & up.
48 pp., softcover, color illust., 8" x 8" or 48 pp., hardcover, color illust., 8¼" x 8¼"

For pricing information, to place an order, or to request a free catalog, contact:

217 Fifth Avenue North • Suite 200 • Minneapolis, MN 55401-1299
toll-free 800.735.7323 • local 612.338.2068 • fax 612.337.5050
help4kids@freespirit.com • www.freespirit.com